Birds and Botanicals

A color Therapy Coloring Book

By

Kim Jordan Blair

I would like to thank my dear friend Mary Ann Morrongiello Manders for coloring the bonnet on the cover of this book.

I would also like to thank my good friend Renee Kritzer for coloring the Peacock on the cover of this book.

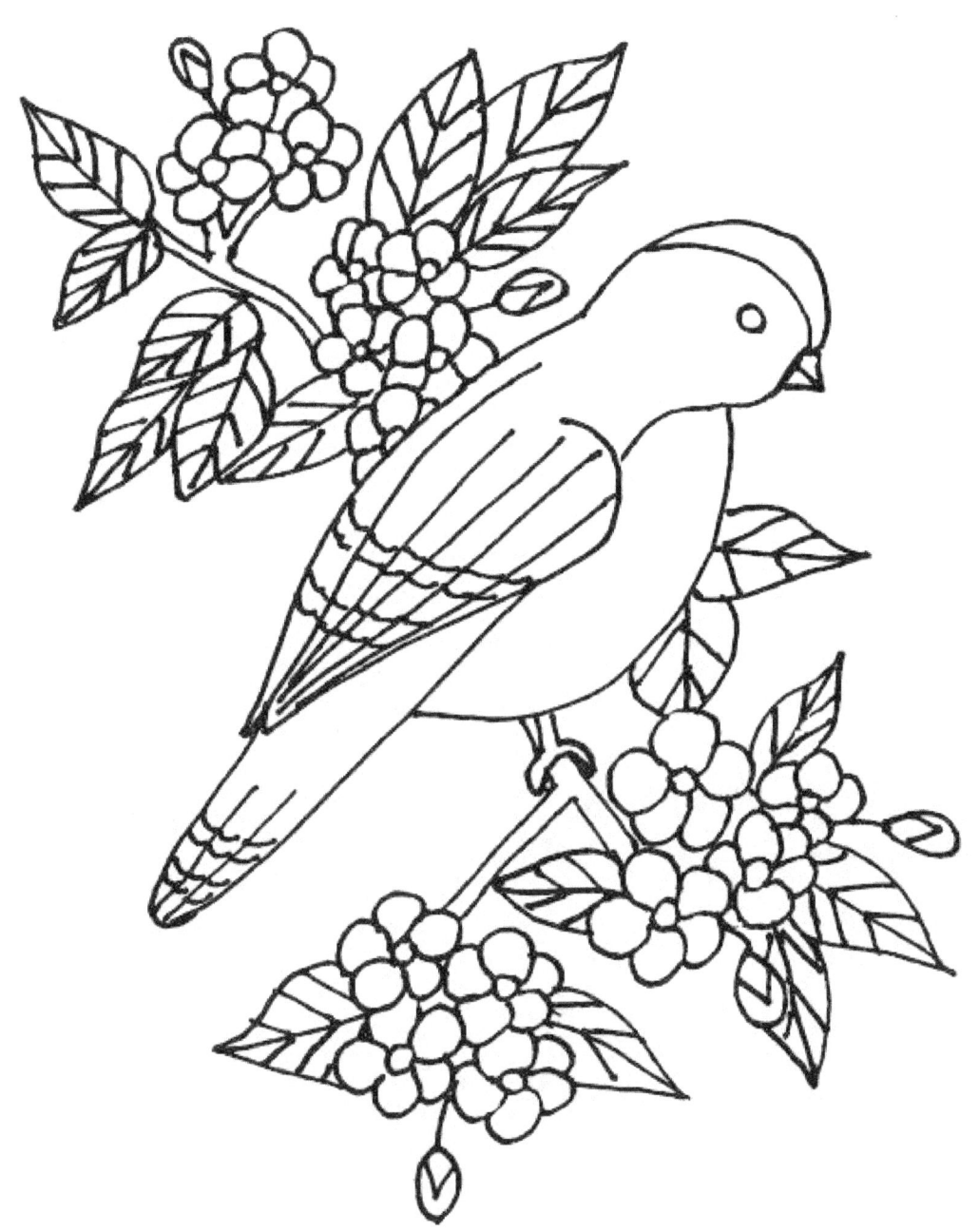

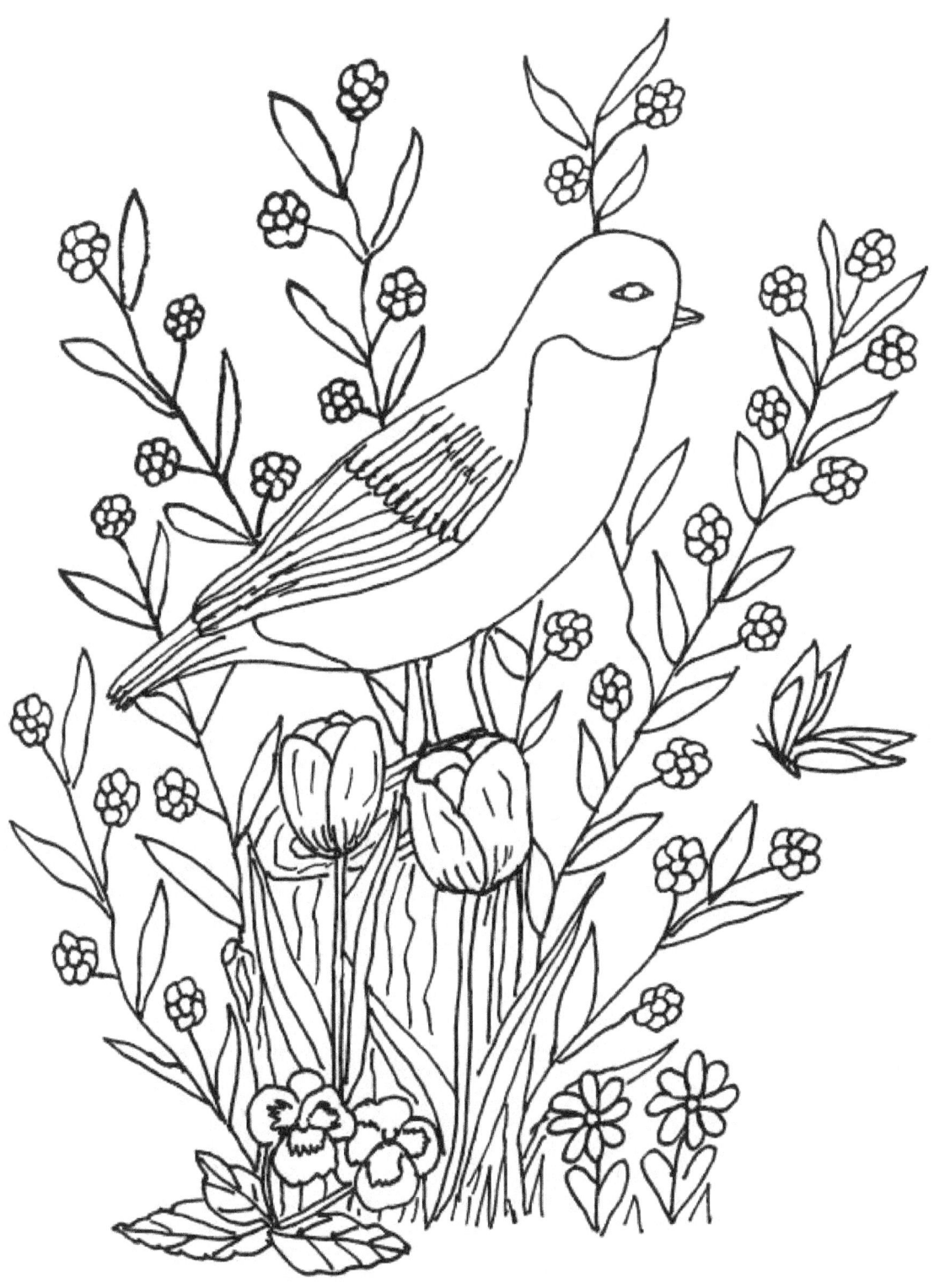

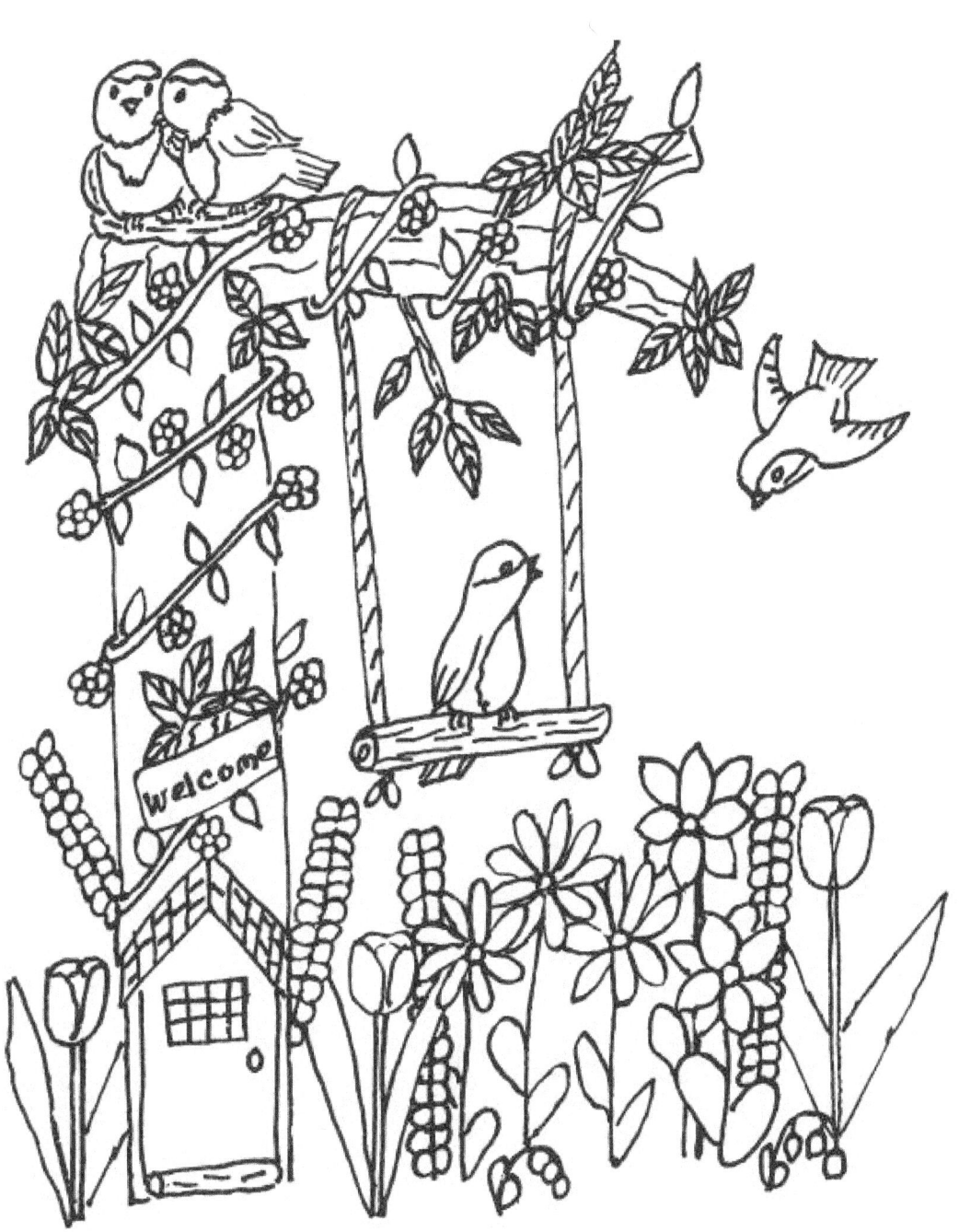

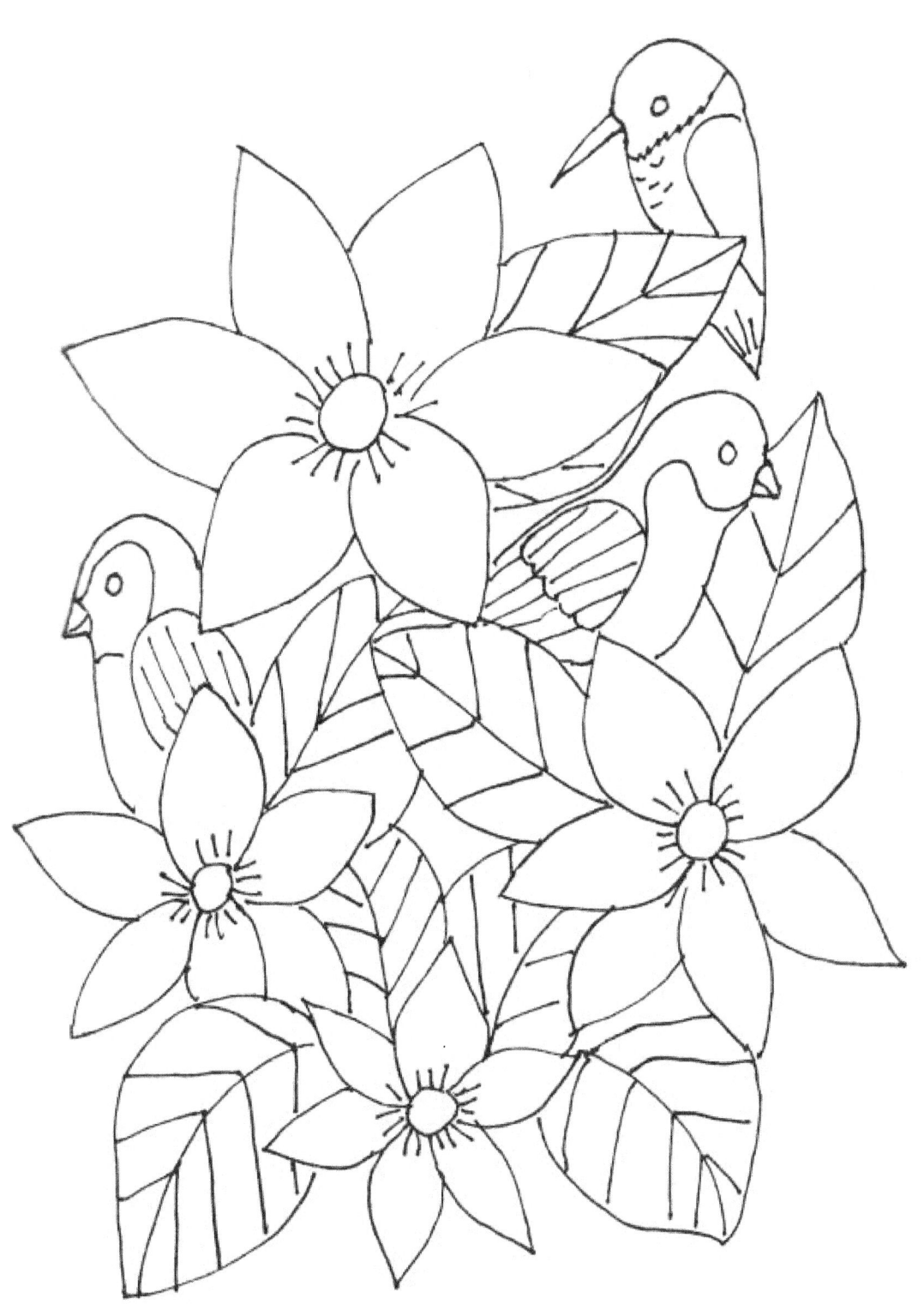

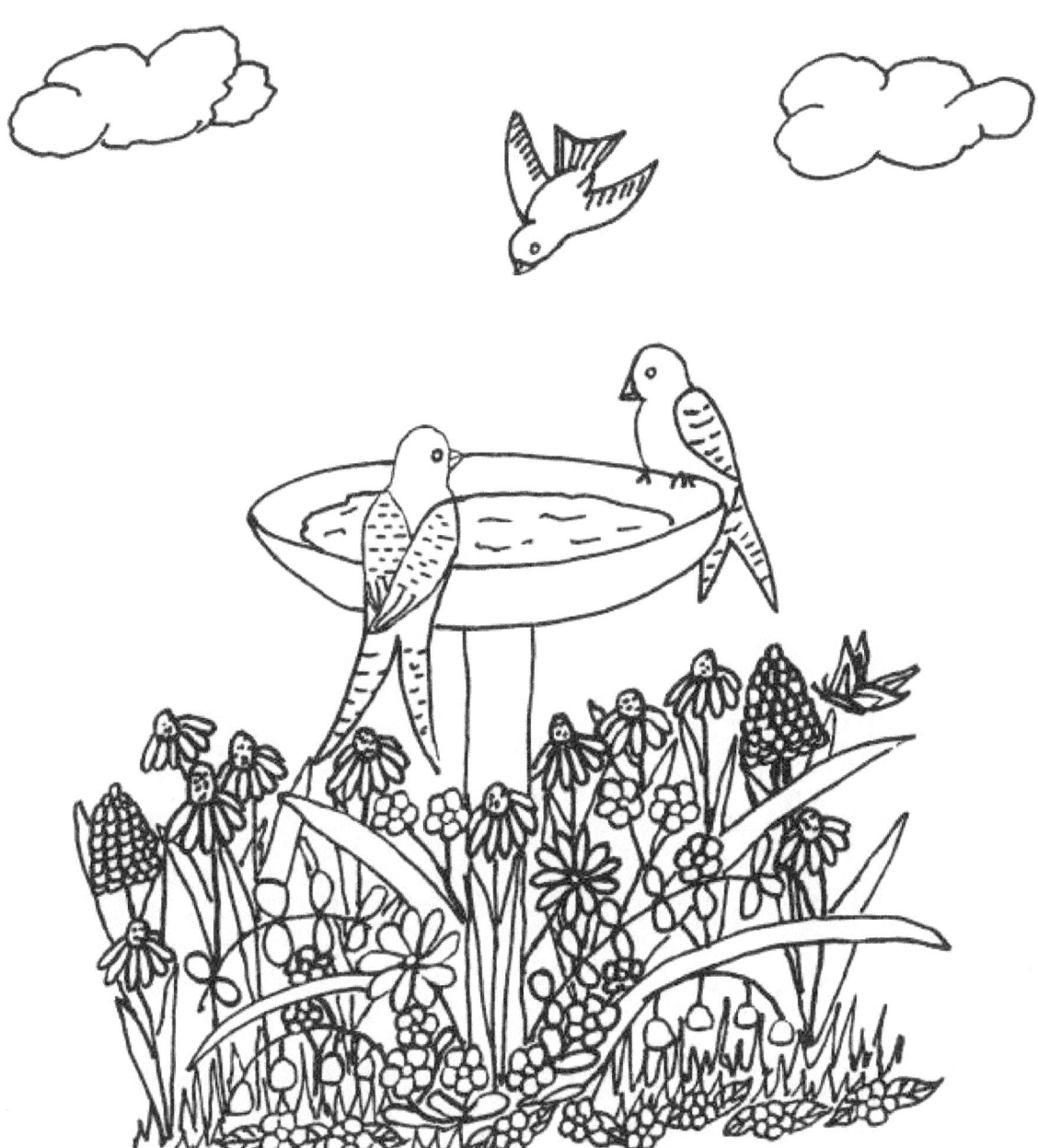

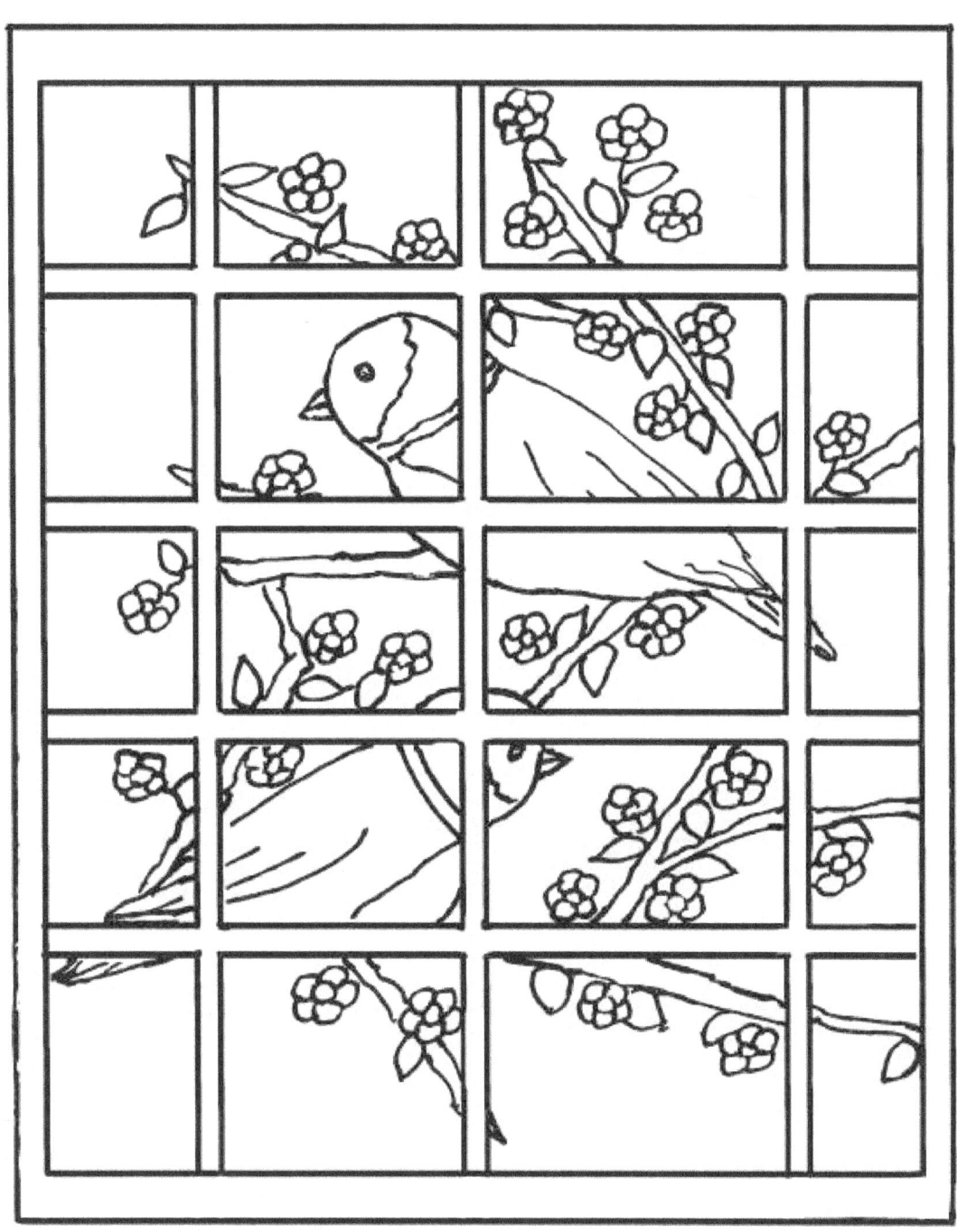

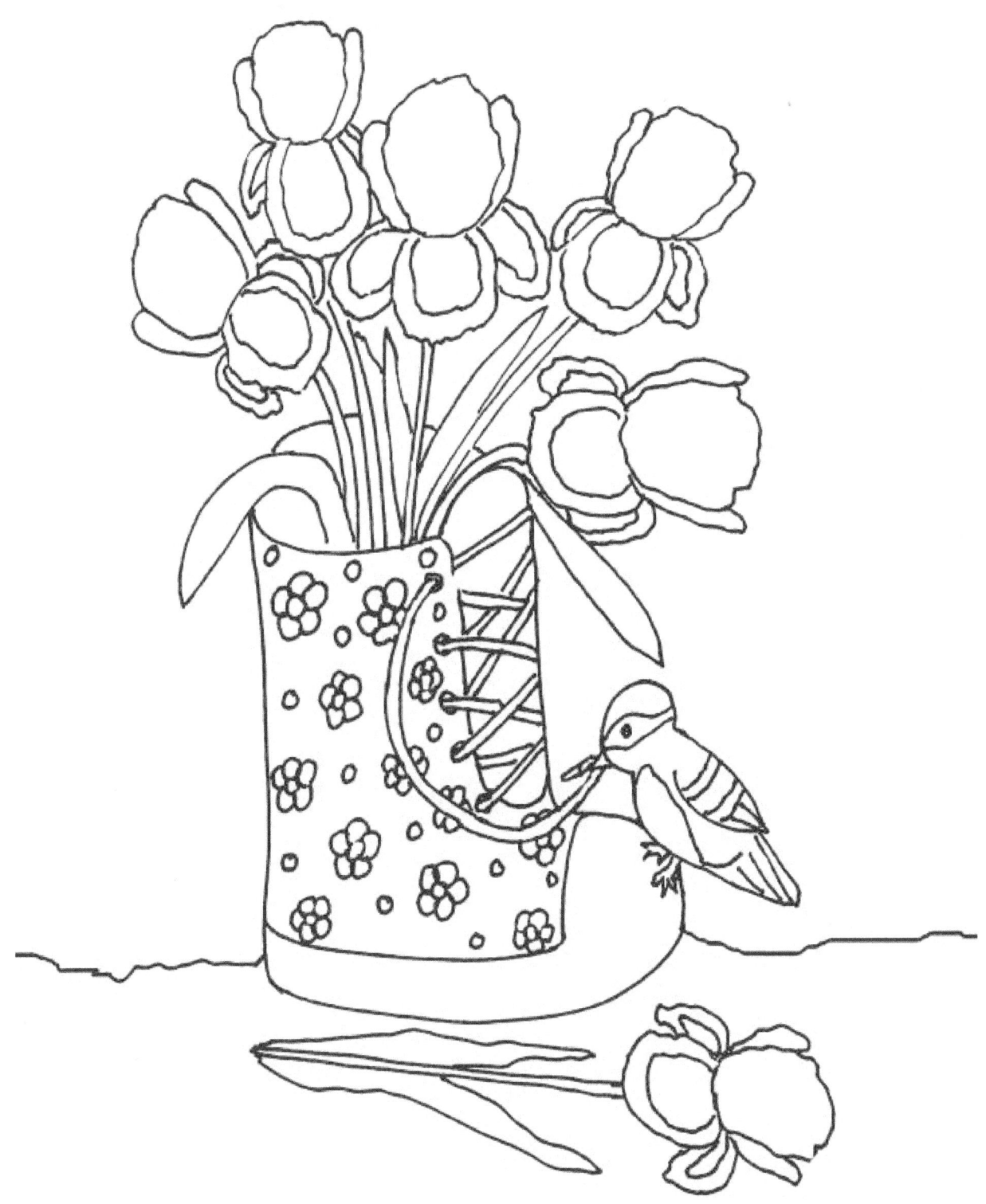

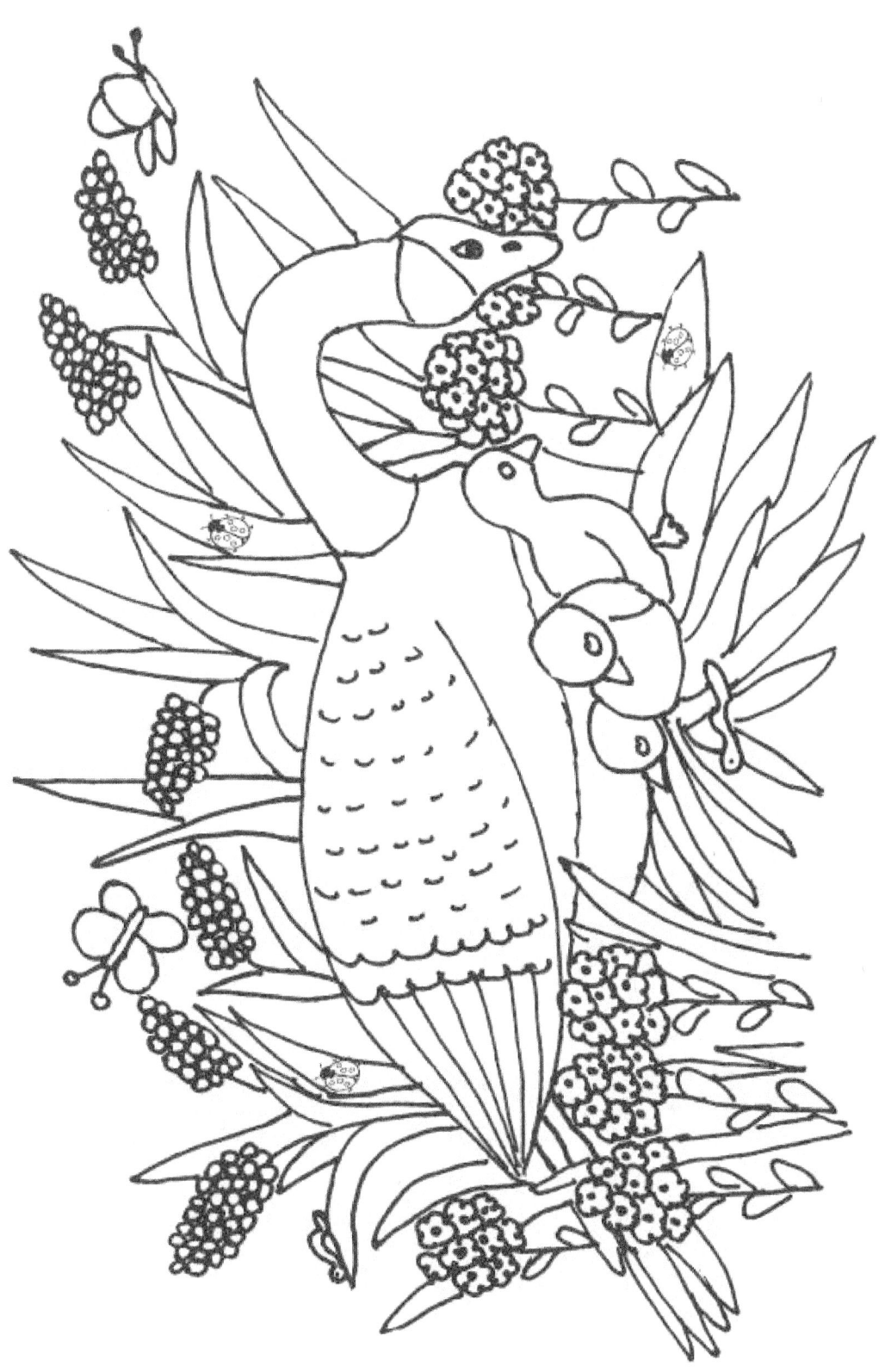

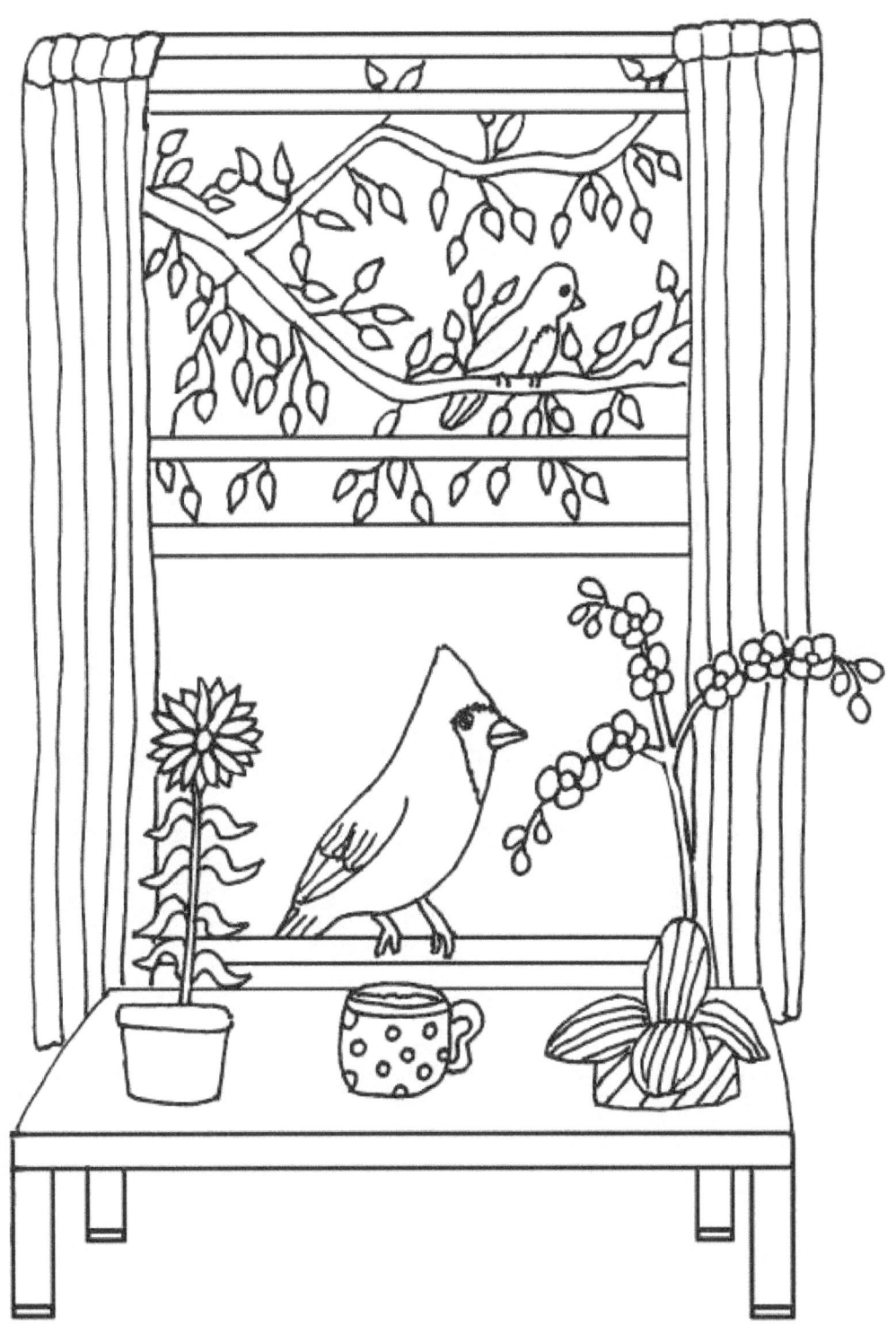

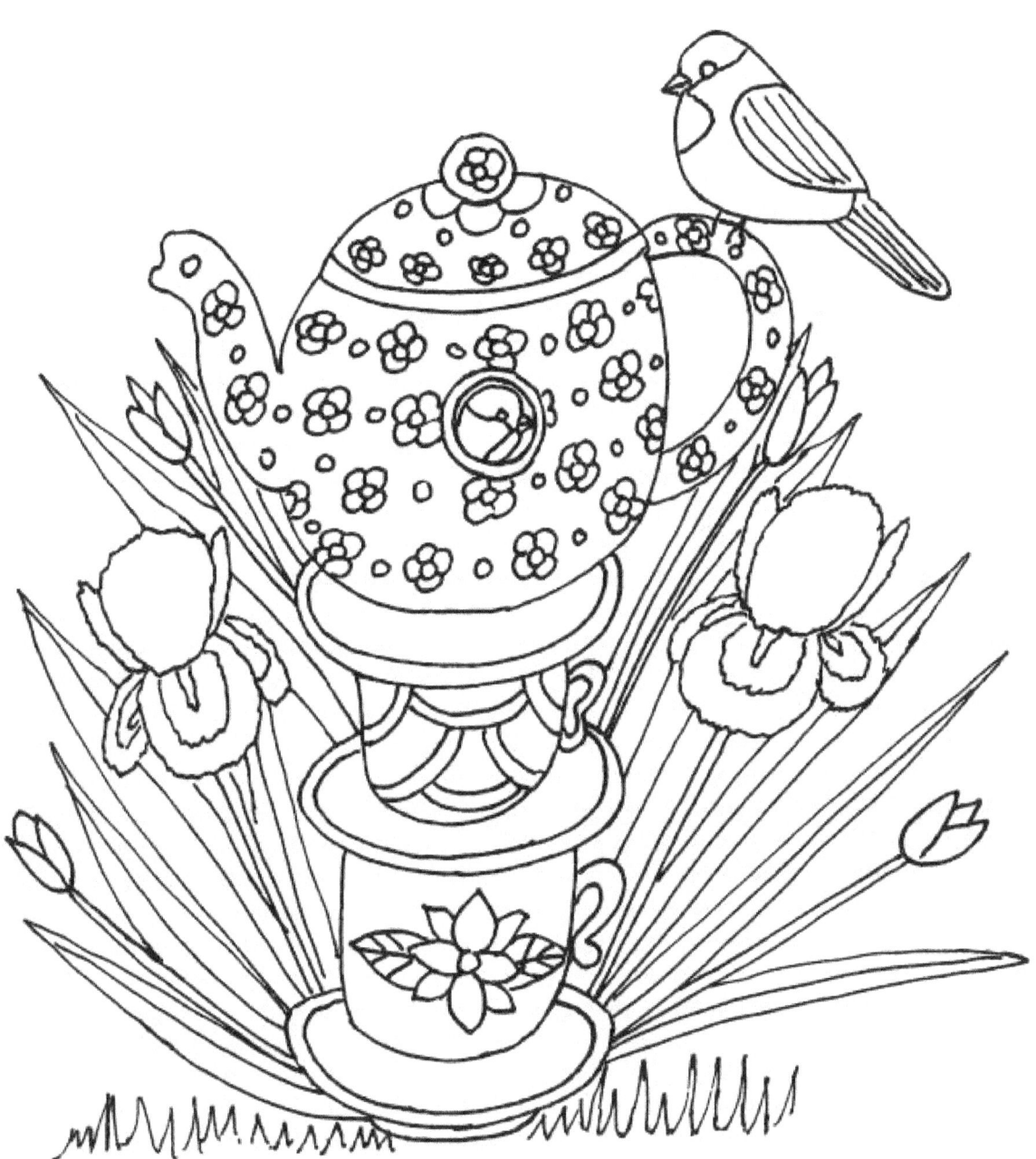

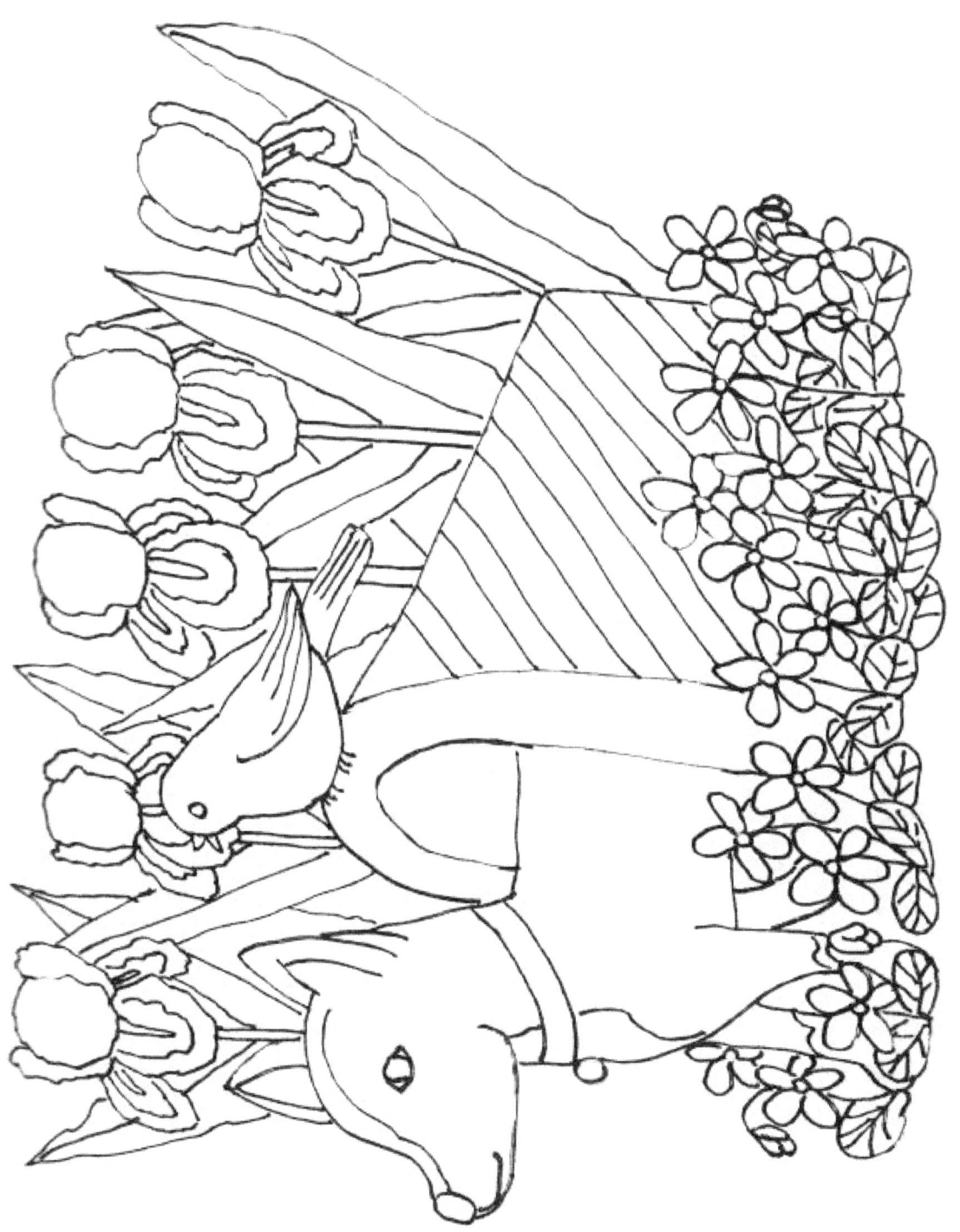

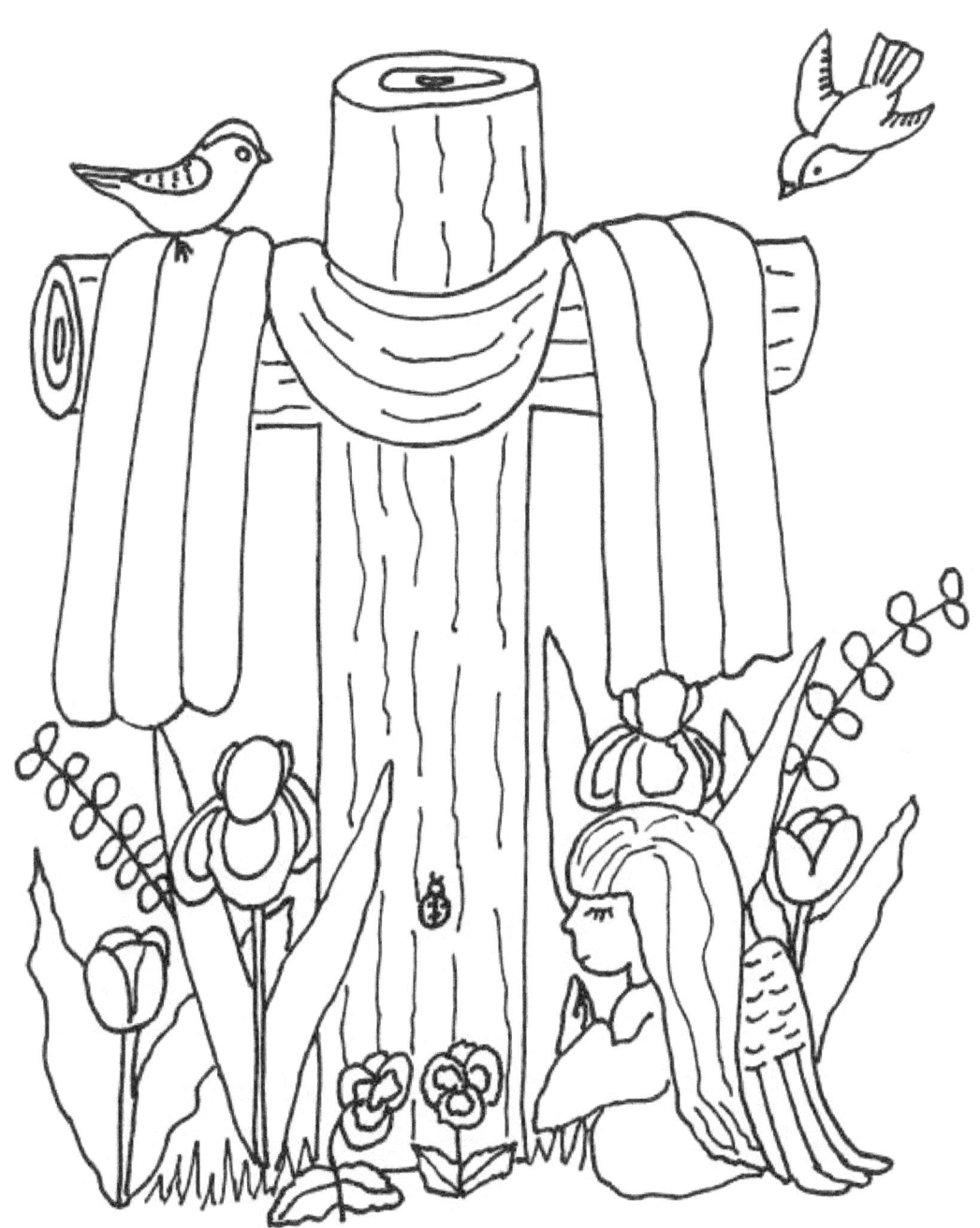

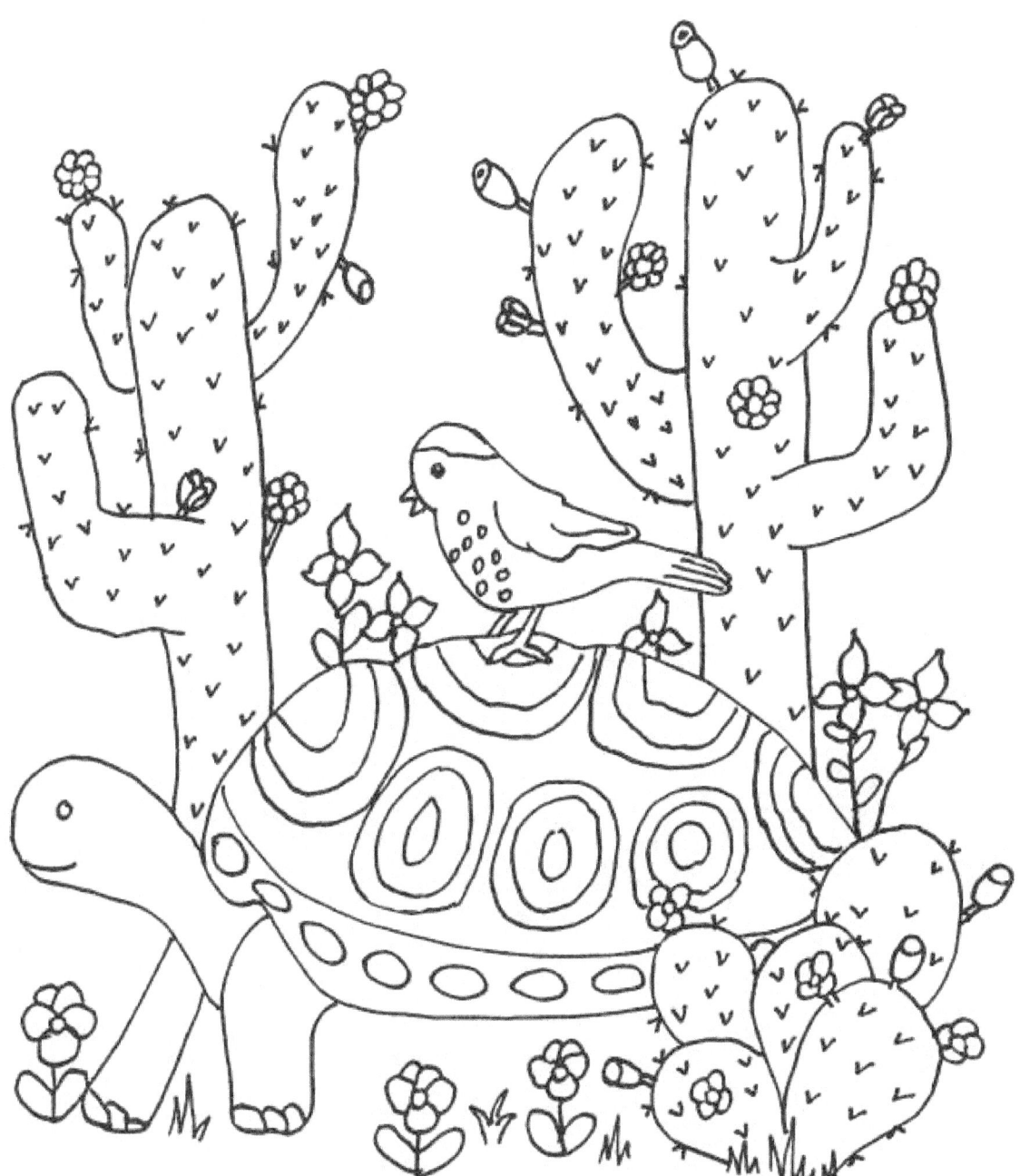

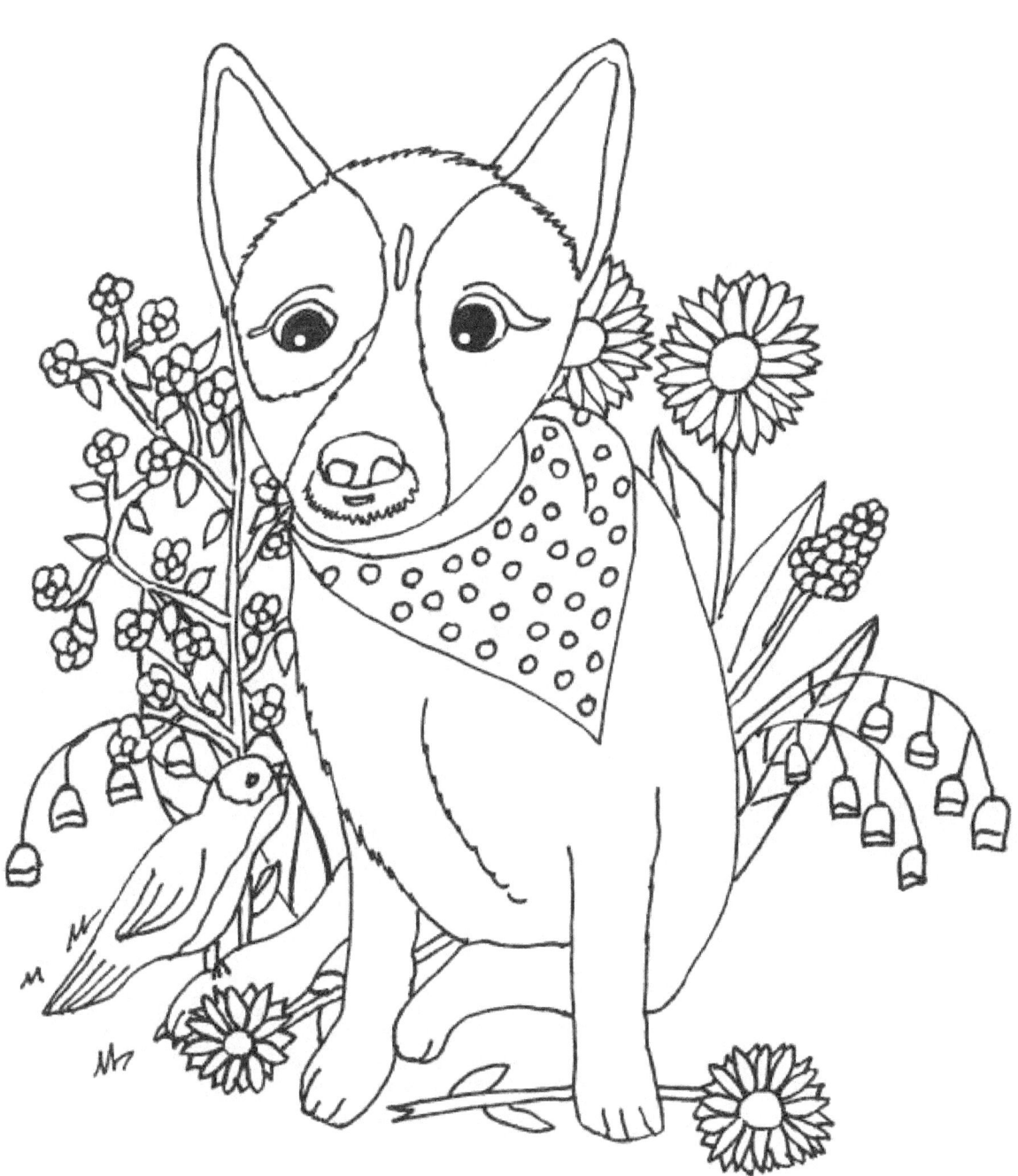

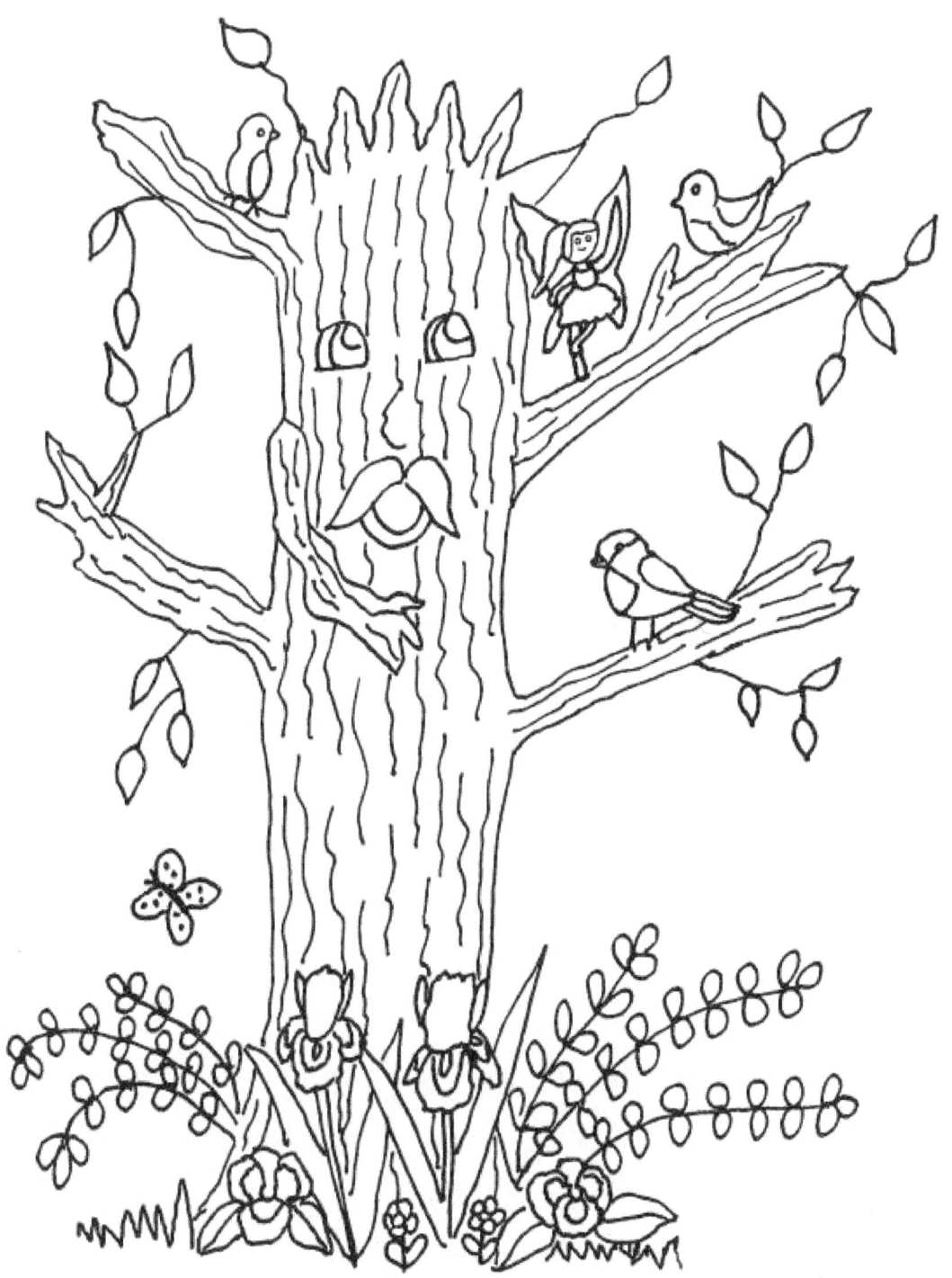

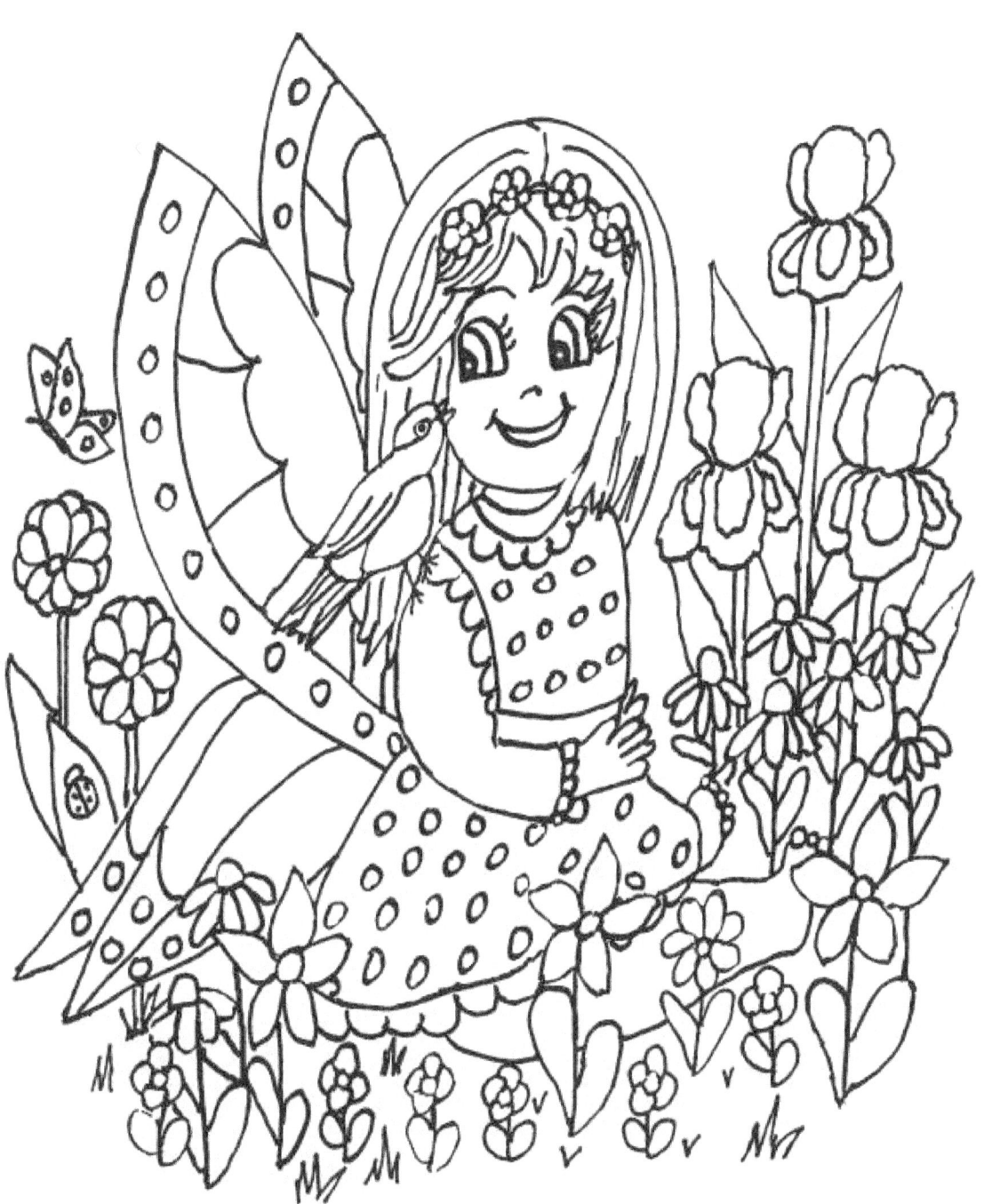

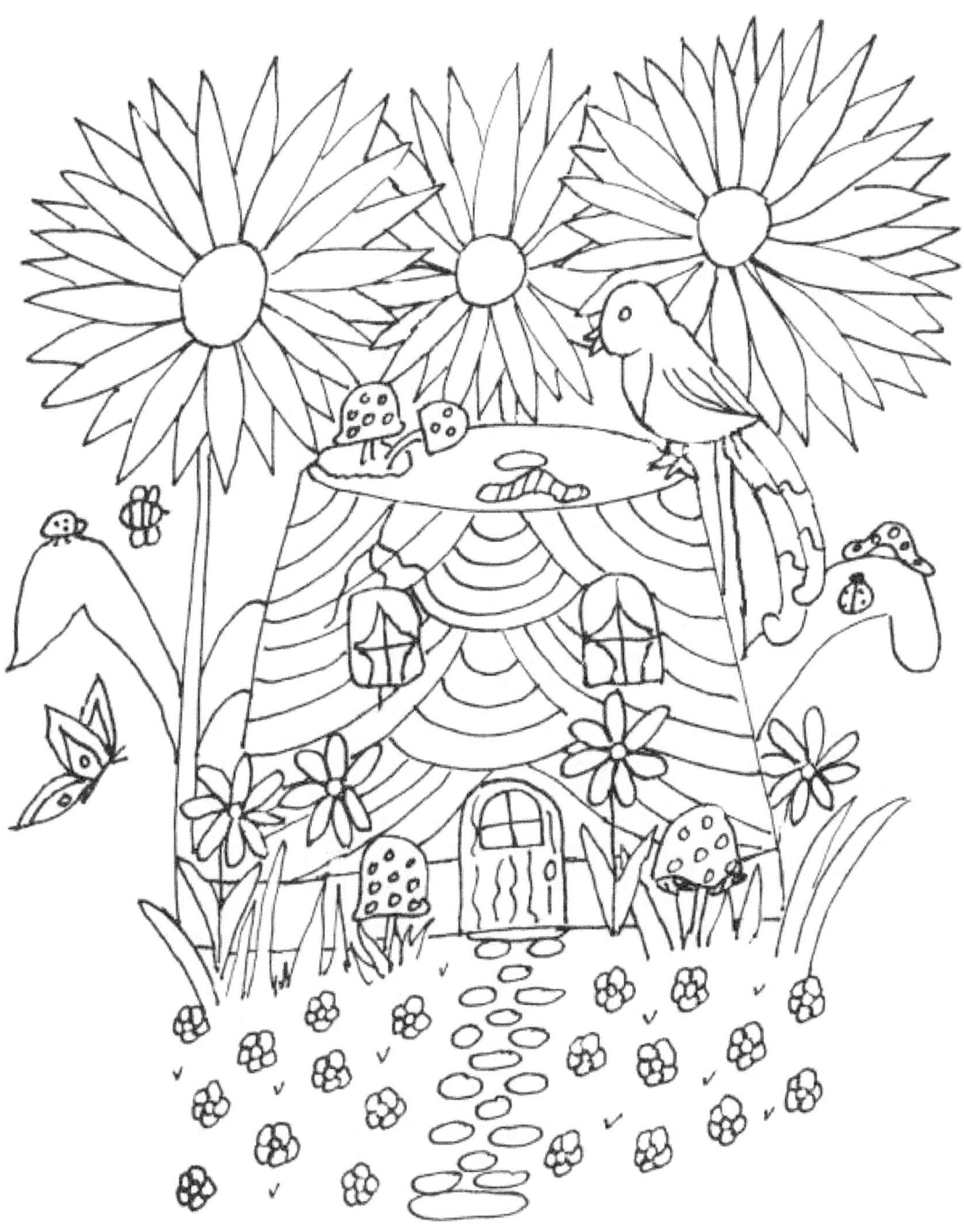

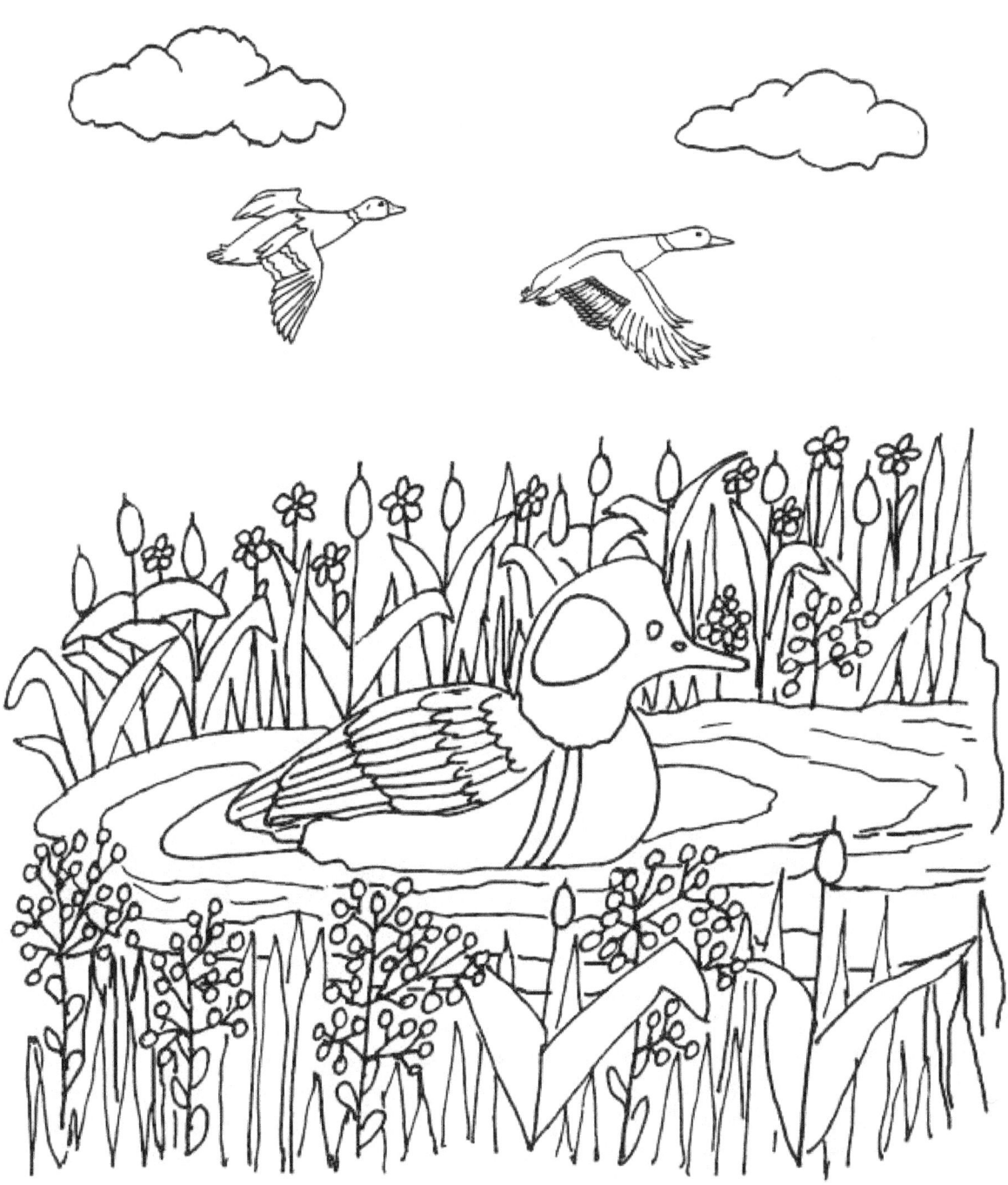

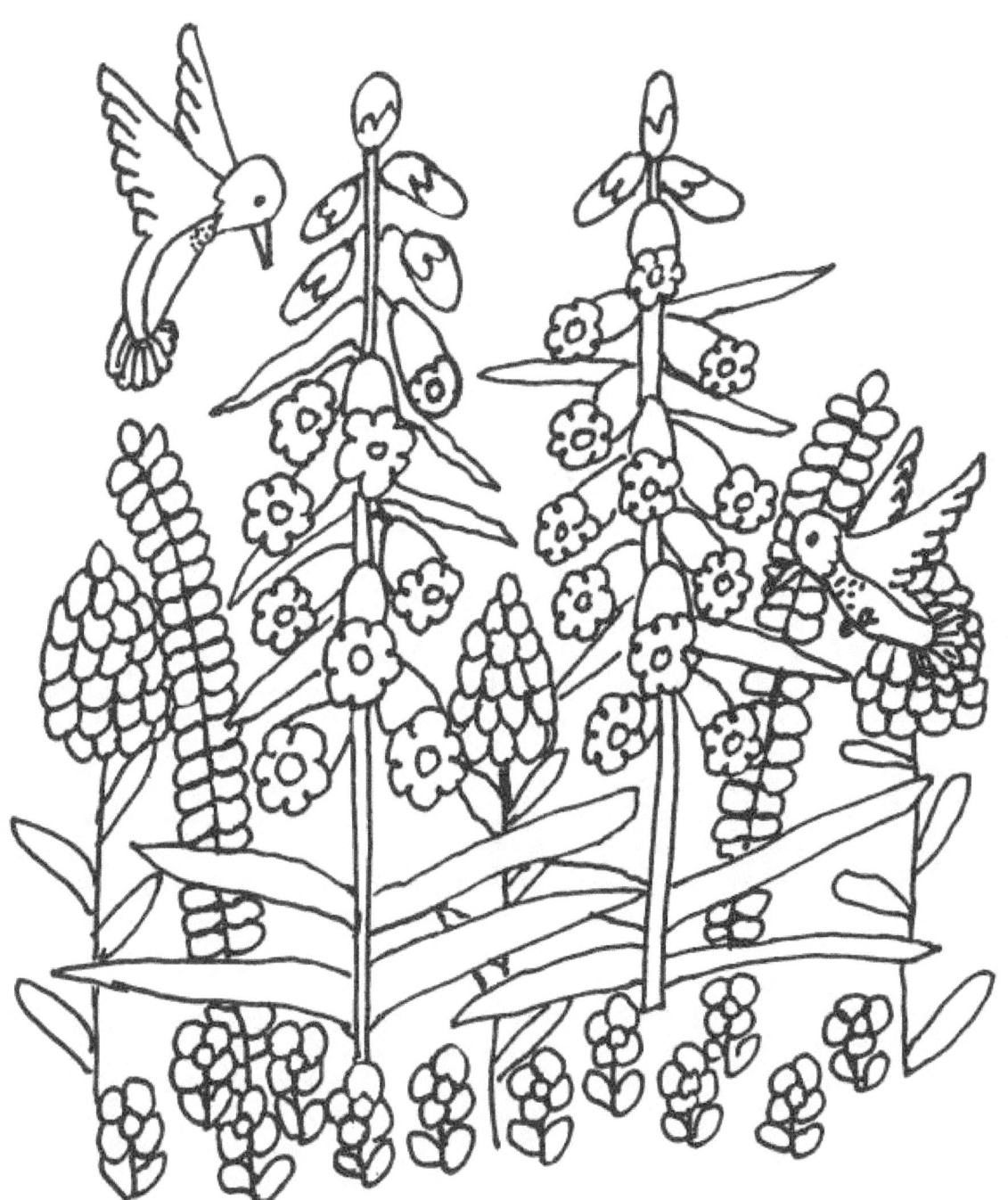

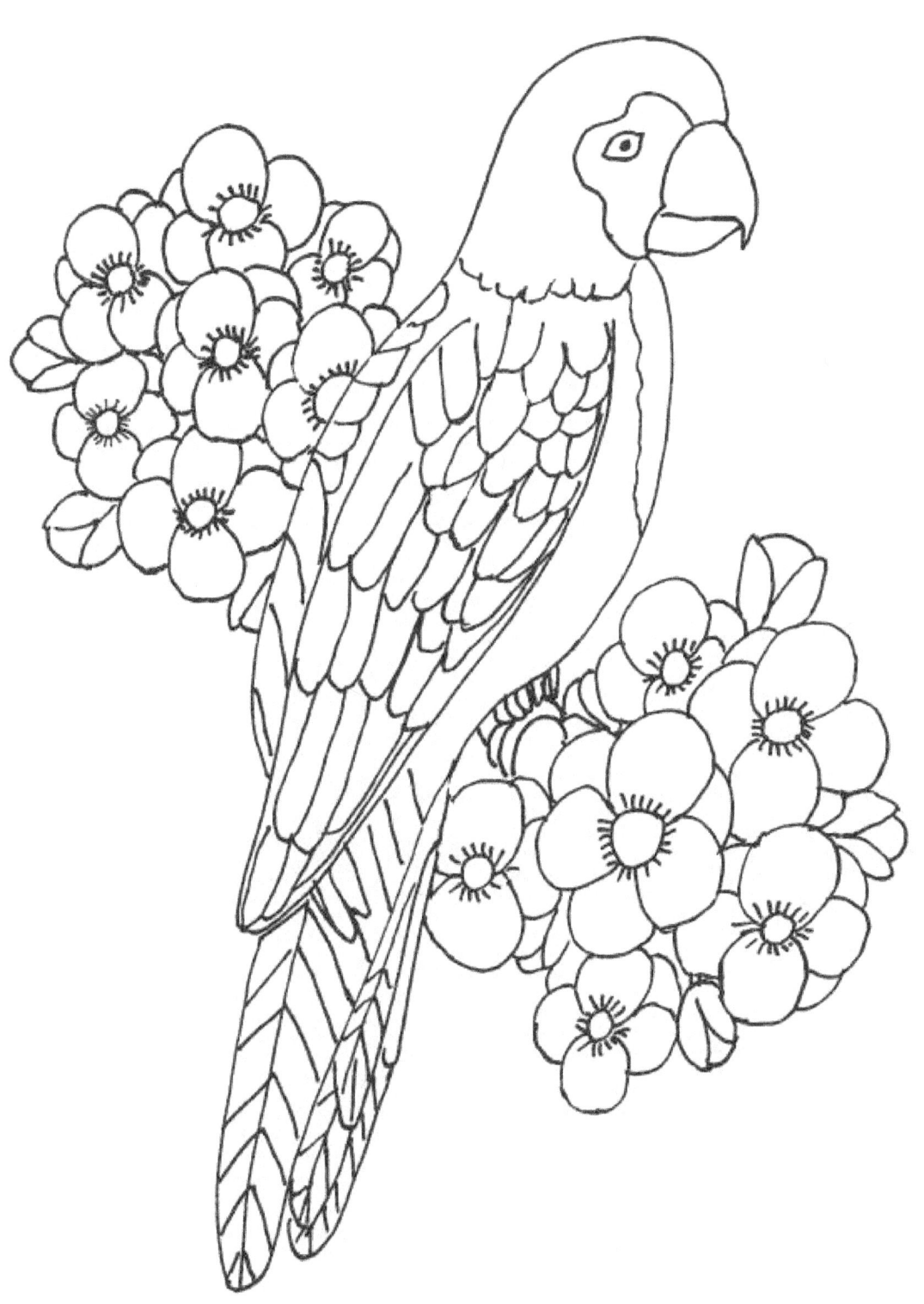

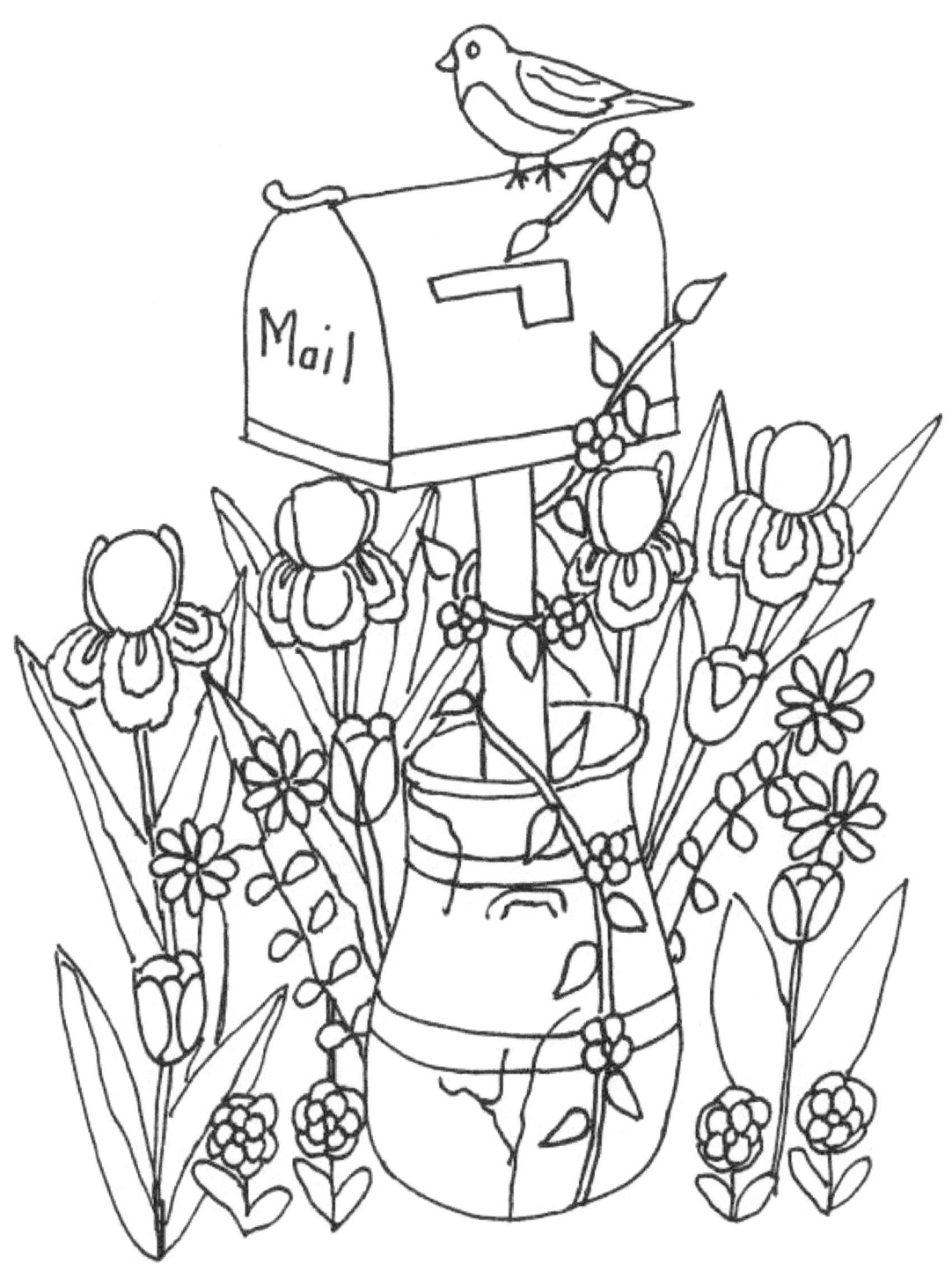

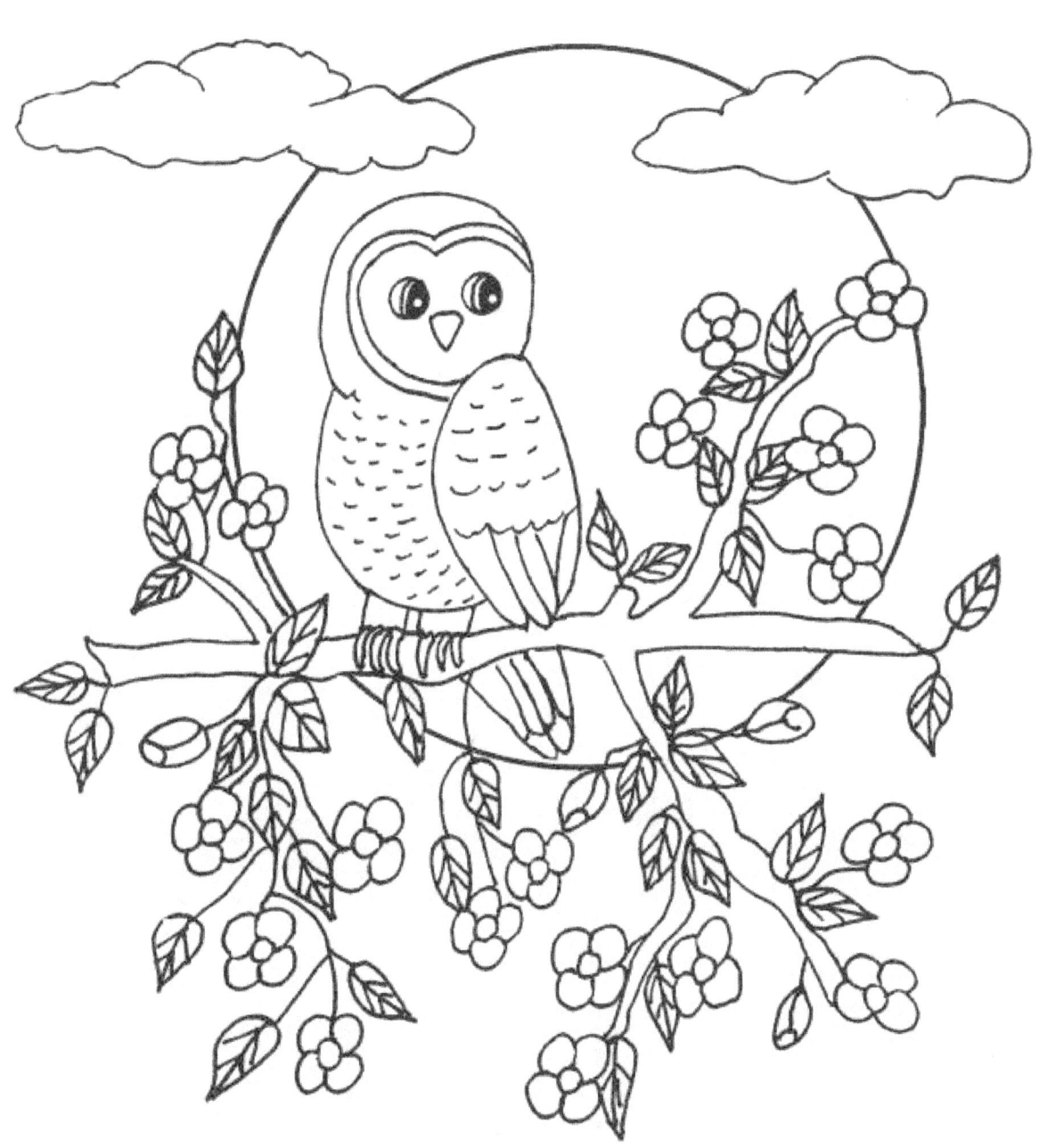

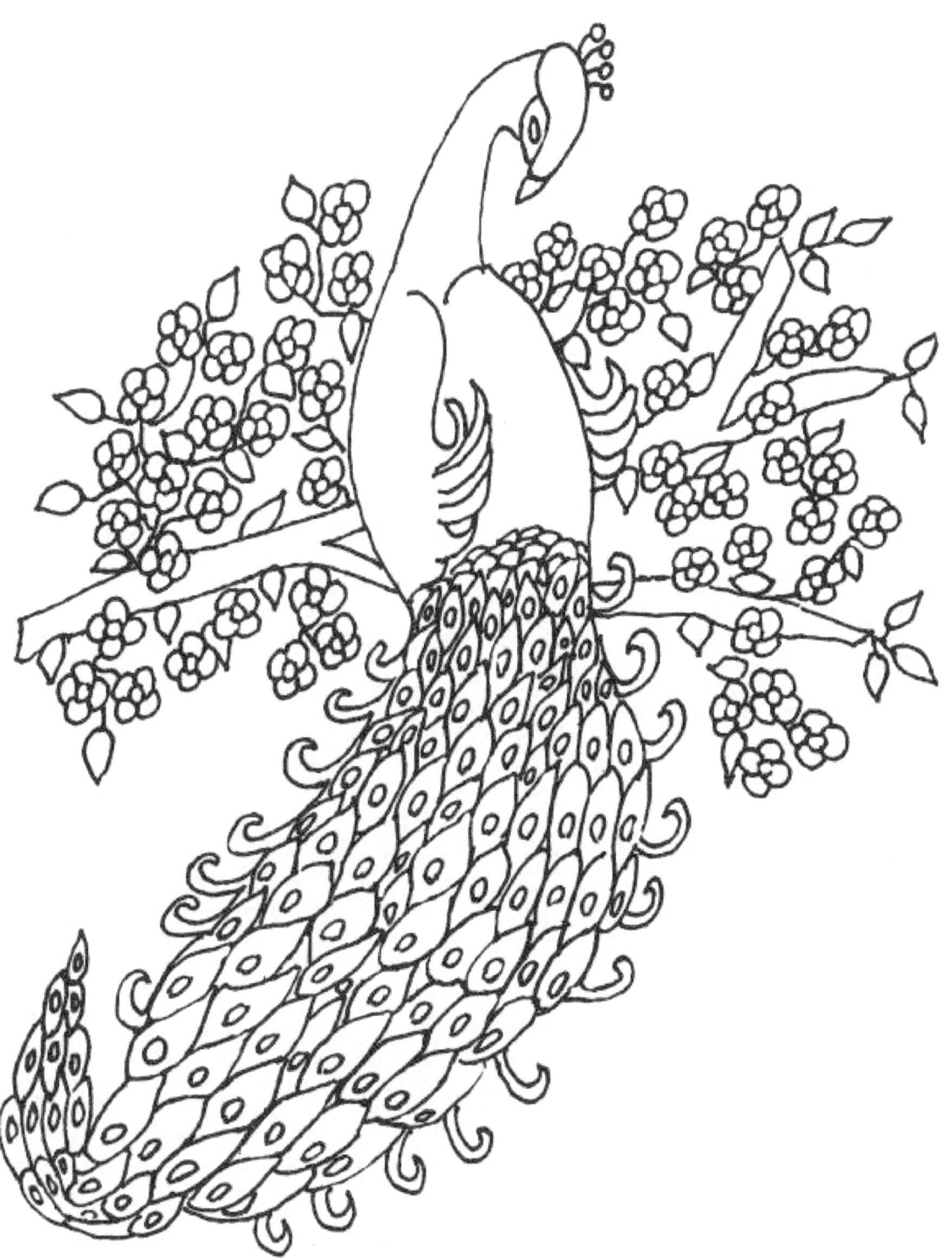

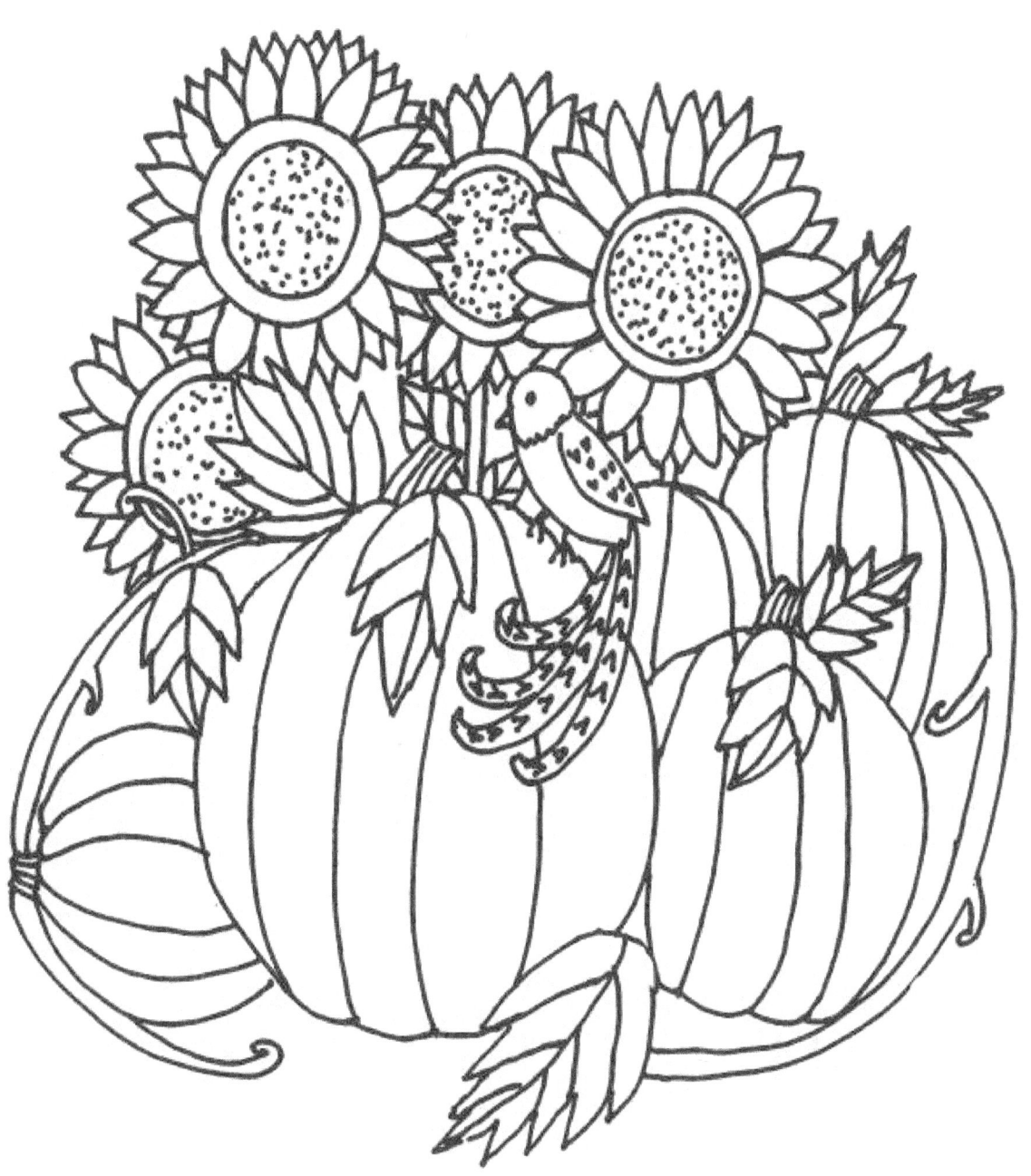

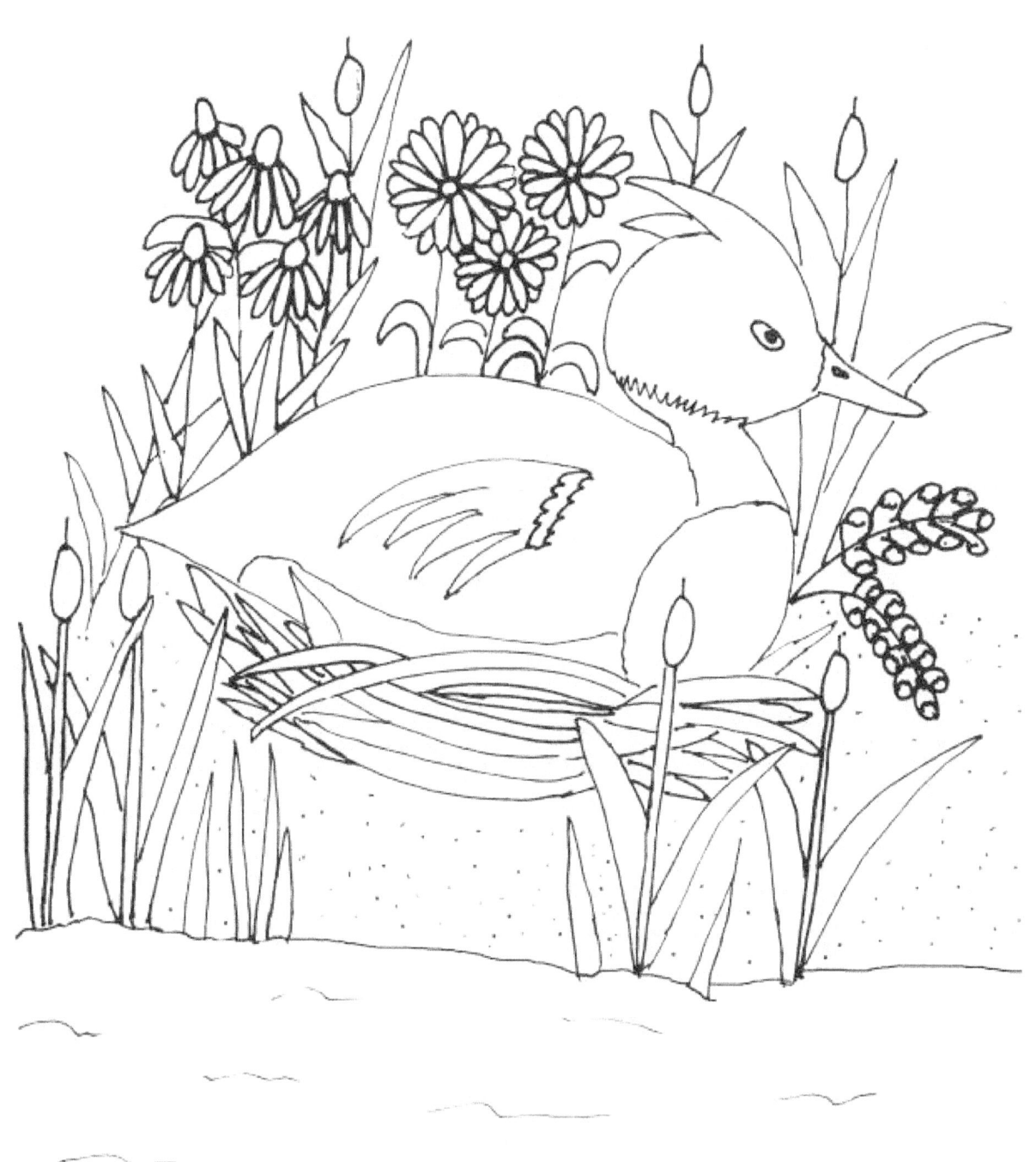

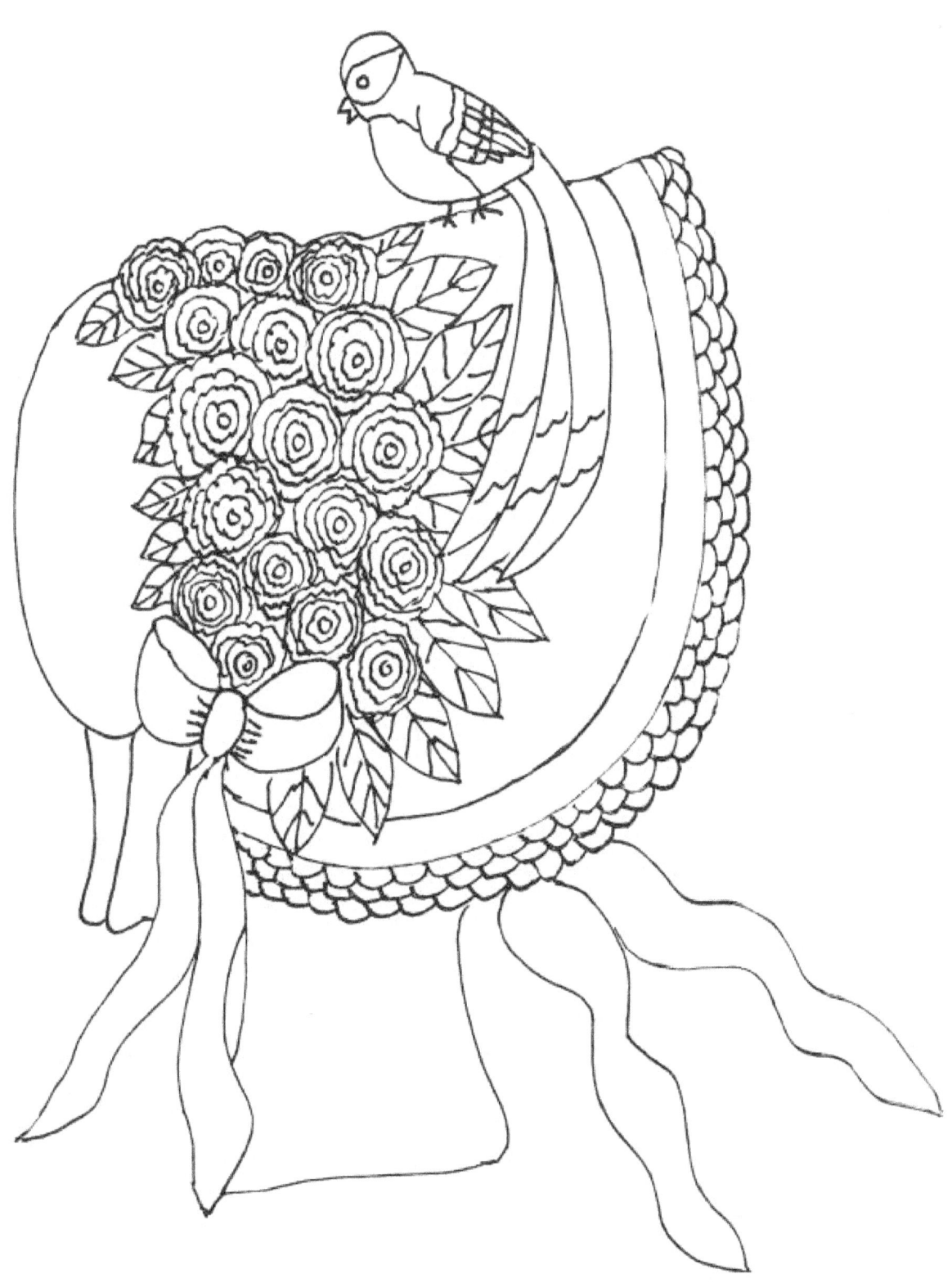

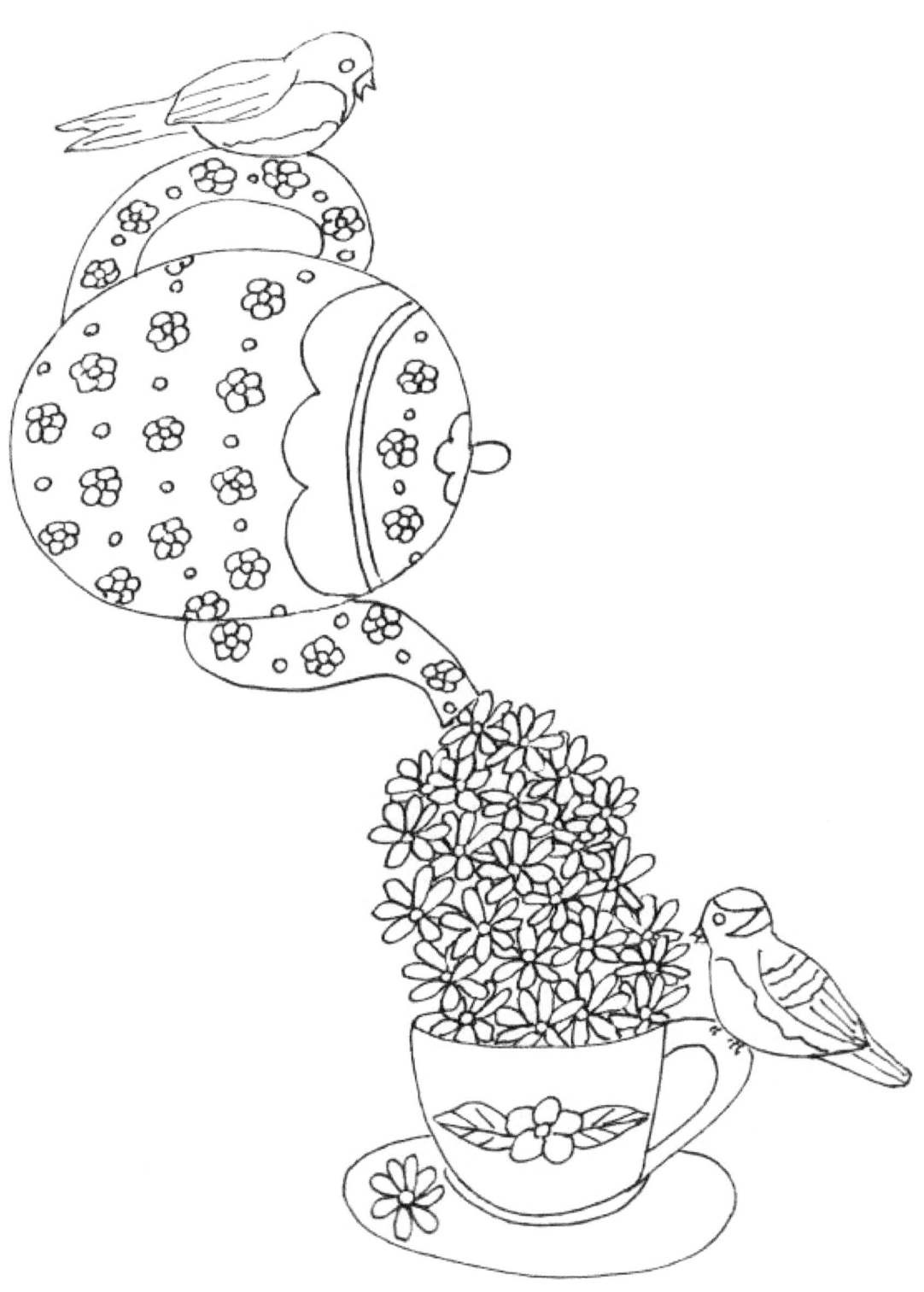

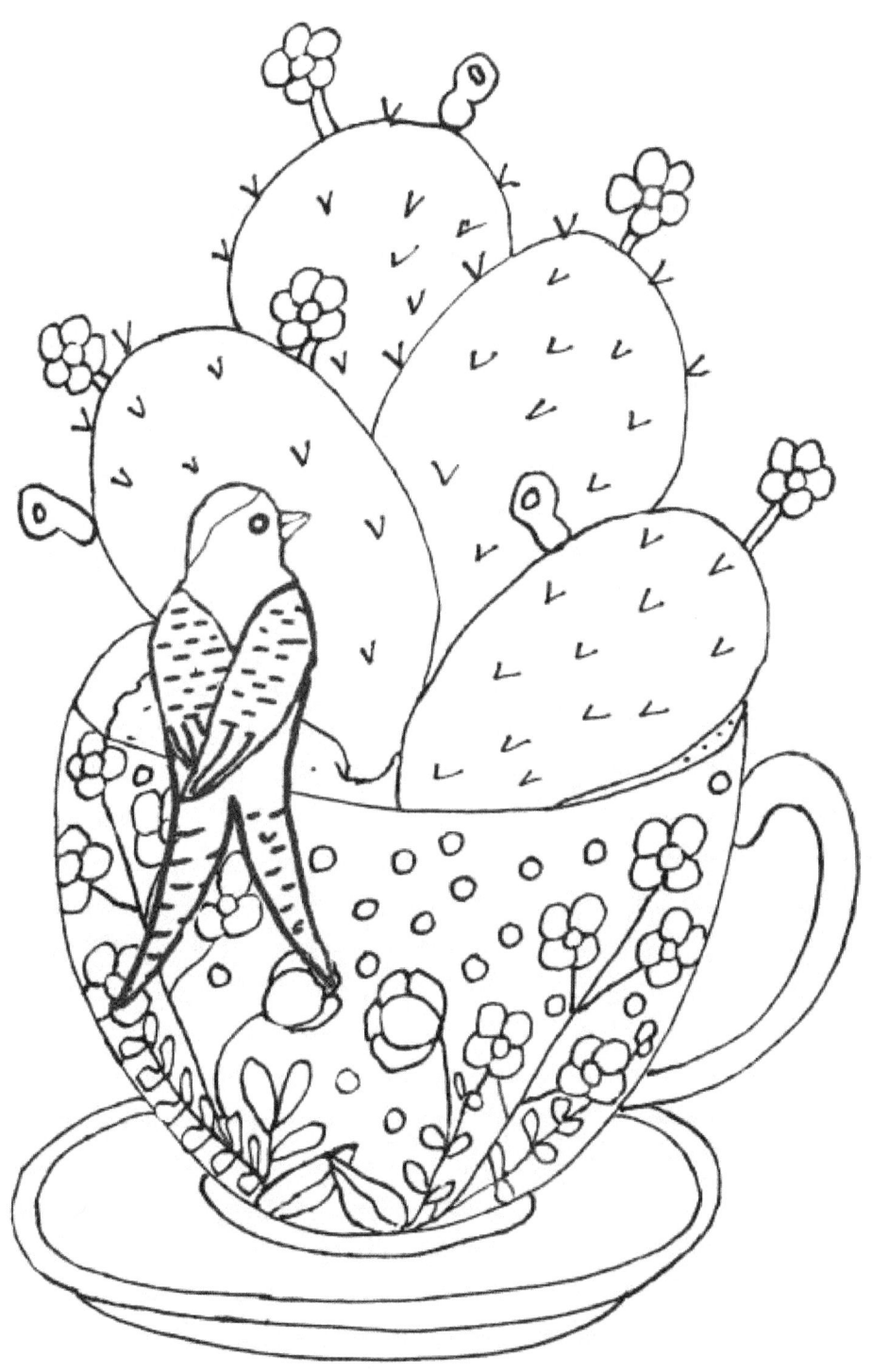

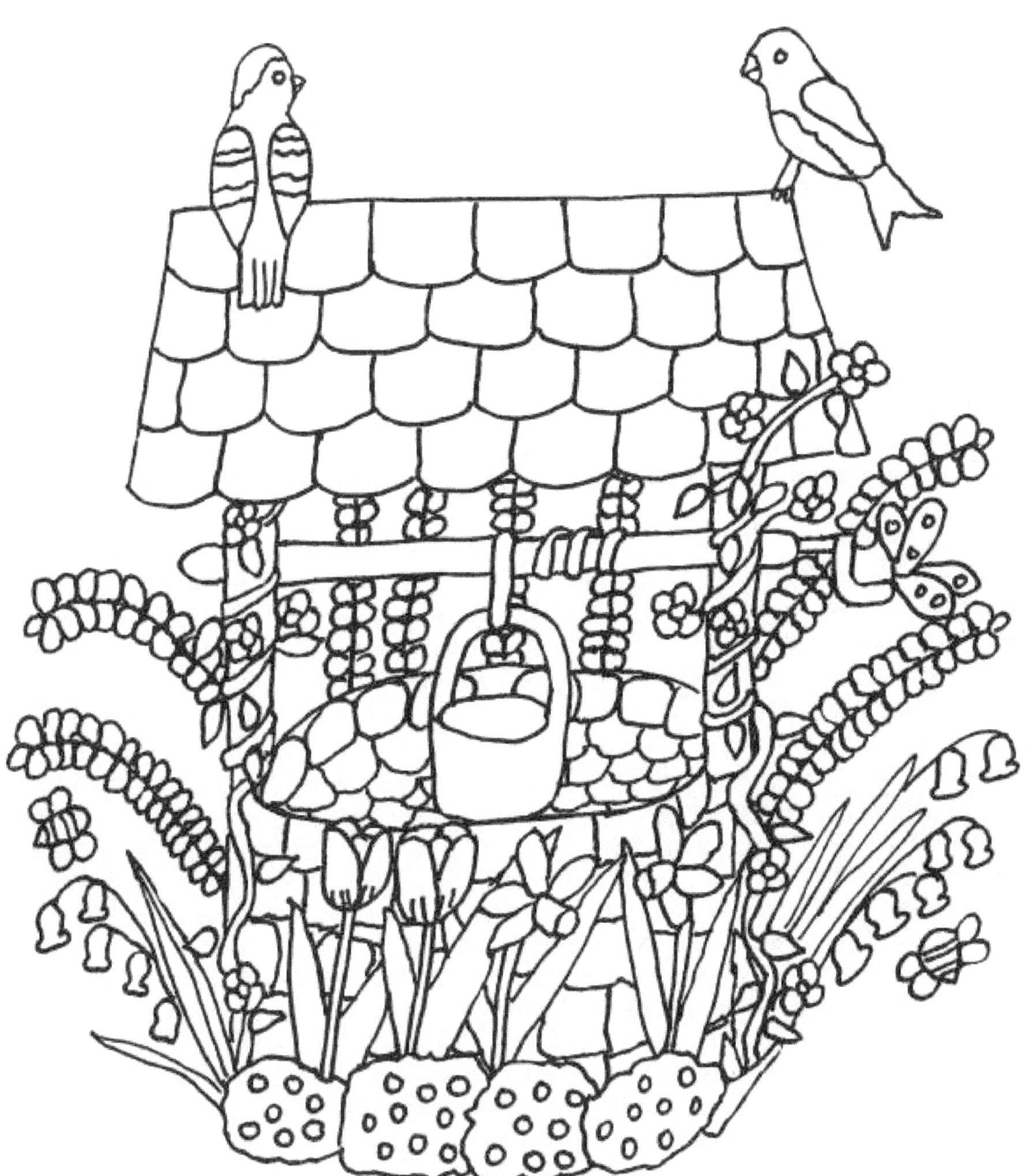

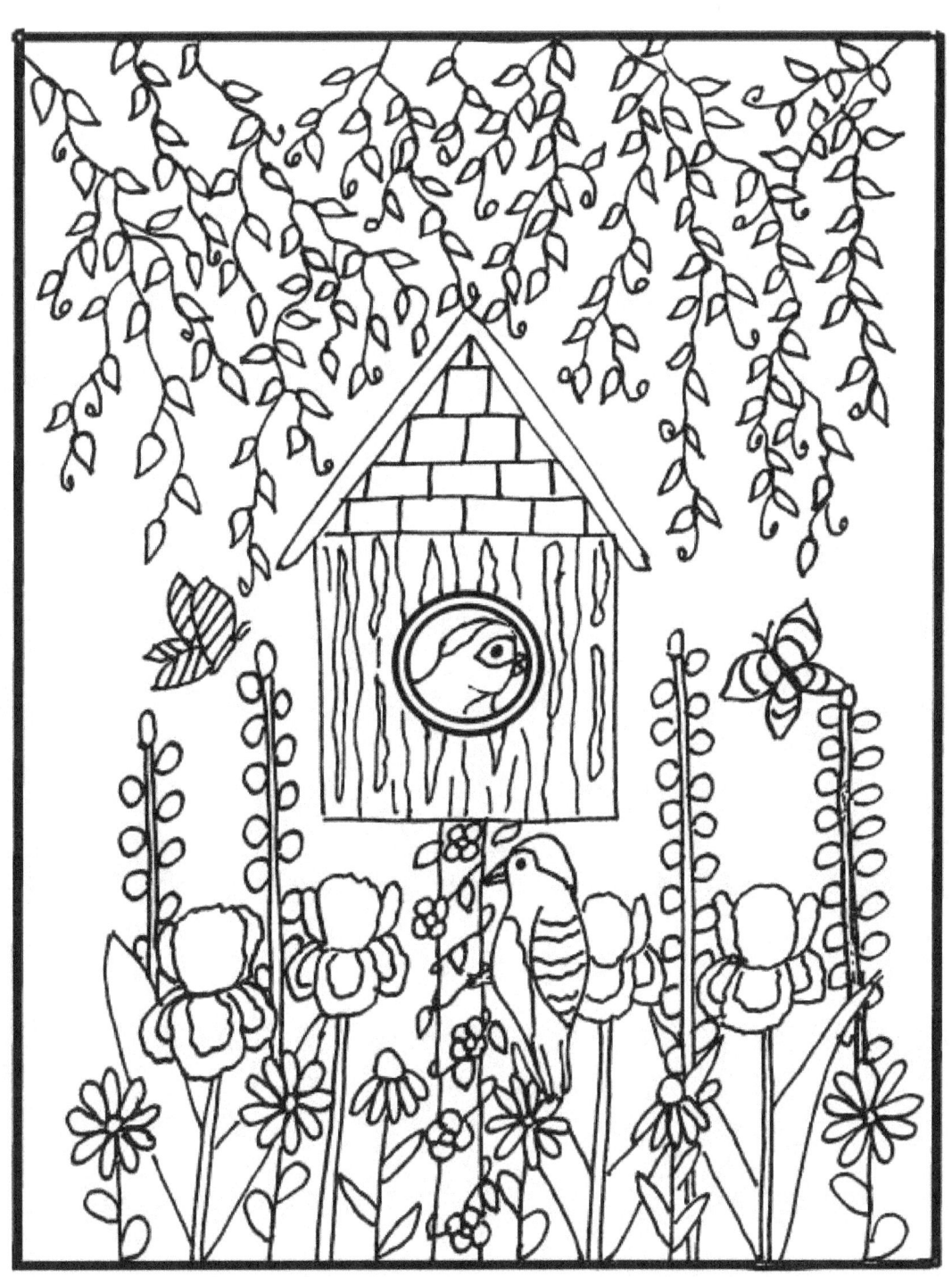

www.ingramcontent.com/pod-product-compliance
Lightning Source LLC
Chambersburg PA
CBHW081121240526
45470CB00019B/2839